# 501
## Word Analogy Questions

# 501

## Word Analogy Questions

LEARNINGEXPRESS

NEW YORK

Library of Congress Cataloging-in-Publication Data:

501 word analogy questions / LearningExpress.—1st ed.
    p. cm.
  ISBN 1-57685-422-1
  1. English language—Synonyms and antonyms—Problems, exercises, etc.
2. Vocabulary—Problems, exercises, etc.  I. LearningExpress (Organization)
  PE1591 .A24 2002
  428.1'076—dc21

                                                          2002006843



Printed in the United States of America
9  8  7  6  5  4  3  2  1
First Edition

ISBN 1-57685-422-1

For more information or to place an order, contact LearningExpress at:
  900 Broadway
  Suite 604
  New York, NY 10003

Or visit us at:
  www.learnatest.com

**The LearningExpress Skill Builder in Focus Writing Team** is comprised of experts in test preparation, as well as educators and teachers who specialize in language arts and math.

*LearningExpress Skill Builder in Focus Writing Team*

Brigit Dermott
Freelance Writer
English Tutor, New York Cares
New York, New York

Sandy Gade
Project Editor
LearningExpress
New York, New York

Kerry McLean
Project Editor
Math Tutor
Shirley, New York

William Recco
Middle School Math Teacher, Grade 8
New York Shoreham/Wading River School District
Math Tutor
St. James, New York

Colleen Schultz
Middle School Math Teacher, Grade 8
Vestal Central School District
Math Tutor
Vestal, New York

# Contents

# Introduction

**Welcome to 501 Word Analogy Questions!** This book is designed to help you prepare for the verbal and reasoning sections of many assessment and entrance exams. By completing the exercises in this book, you will develop the skills necessary to tackle each type of analogy question.

Many standardized tests—including high school entrance exams, the SATs, civil service exams, the GREs, and others—use analogy questions to test both logic and reasoning skills and word knowledge. These questions ask test takers to identify relationships between pairs of words. In order to solve analogy questions, you must first have a clear understanding of the words' definitions and then use that understanding to determine how the words are related.

Analogy questions are often described as "blank is to blank as blank is to blank." So for example, puppy : dog :: kitten : _____, is read "puppy is to dog as kitten is to blank." The answer is, of course, "cat." However, the "blank is to blank" format does not really answer the question precisely. More accurately, you might describe the relationship between puppy and dog as "a puppy is a young dog." To

determine the missing word, you might say "a kitten is a young . . . "
The key to solving an analogy question is to precisely describe the
relationship between the pair of words and then apply the same relationship to determine which word completes the analogy.

Most analogy questions rely on your ability to deduce the correct
relationship between words and to draw logical conclusions about the
possible answer choices. For example in the question "Sherpa : Tibet
:: Massai : _____," you can probably guess the correct answer from
the following choices—**a.** mountain, **b.** bicycle, **c.** Kenya, **d.** desert—
even if you do not know the exact meaning of the words in the question. The correct answer is Kenya—Sherpa are people who live in
Tibet and Massai are people who live in Kenya. Even if you were
unable to describe the relationship between the words because they
are unfamiliar, you could probably see that Kenya is the only country offered as a choice. As you know that Tibet , a country, is the second half of the first pair, you can deduce that a country is necessary
to complete the second pair.

The relationships that are found in analogy questions fall into sev-
eral general types.

- Part to Whole. In this type of question, a pair of words
  consists of a part and a whole. For example, spoke :
  wheel. A spoke is part of a wheel.
- Type and Category. These questions use pairs of words in
  which one word is a specific type in a general category.
  For example, orange : citrus. An orange is a type of citrus.
- Degree of Intensity. These questions test your ability to
  discern nuance of meaning among pairs of words. For
  example, shower : monsoon. A shower is light rainfall and
  a monsoon is heavy rainfall.
- Function. These questions pair words that are related
  through function. For example, hammer : build. A
  hammer is used to build.
- Manner. This type of analogy describes the manner, way,
  or style by which an action is accomplished. For example,

shamble : walk. Shamble means to walk in an awkward manner.

- Symbol or representation. These questions pair words in which one word is the symbol of the other. For example, dove : peace. A dove is a symbol of peace.
- Action and significance. In this type of analogy one word describes an action and the other word indicates the significance of the action. For example, cry : sorrow. To cry signifies sorrow.

Analogy questions can also be used to test word knowledge and factual content. Word knowledge questions are generally pairs of synonyms or pairs of antonyms. For example, tardy : _____ :: liberal : generous. Liberal and generous are synonyms, therefore you would look for a synonym of tardy among the answer choices. Factual content questions demand a certain level of general knowledge, and cannot be deduced from the relationship alone. For example:

iron : Fe :: silver : _____
a. Na
b. Cl
c. Ag
d. K

In this case you need to know that the chemical symbol for silver is Ag. Even though these questions require some basic knowledge you can still apply logic to the question. For example, if you know that the chemical name for table salt is NaCl, you can eliminate these two answers. This leaves you with Ag and K. If you happen to know that the French word for silver is *argent*, then Ag would be an excellent educated guess.

There is a final type of analogy question that is purely a logic test. These questions pair seemingly unrelated words. The relationship is found in the arrangement of the letters. For example:

about : bout :: _____ : mend
a. amend
b. near
c. tear
d. dismiss

In this case, the answer is amend because that is the word formed by adding an "a" in front of mend. You will also find scrambled words and anagrams in this category of analogies.

The questions increase in difficulty as you move through each set of exercises. Because this book is designed for many levels of test takers, you may find that some of the more advanced questions are beyond your ability. If you are using this book to study for a high school entrance exam, you may get a number of questions that appear later in a section wrong. Don't worry! If you are getting the earlier questions correct, you are probably in good shape for your test. However, if you are studying for a graduate-level exam such as the GRE or the MAT, the full range of questions presented is appropriate for your level.

The questions in this book can help you prepare for your test in many ways. First, completing these practice exercises will make you familiar with the question format. They will also help you get used to identifying the relationships between pairs of words. In the case of solving analogies, practice really does make perfect. The more comfortable you are with the question format and the more familiar you are with the range of analogy types, the easier this section on your test will become.

Second, your performance on these questions will help you assess your ability and vocabulary level. You may find that you do very well on those questions that require logical deduction to find the correct answer, but that you have trouble with those questions that test word knowledge. In this case, you will know that you need to spend more time improving your vocabulary.

Third, you will become familiar not only with word relationships and word meanings, but you will also learn to spot and disregard wrong answer choices through practice. At first, there may seem to be many different reasons for getting various questions wrong. At closer look, however, there may be a pattern to your wrong answers. Test preparers often spend as much time on wrong answer choices as they do the right answer. For instance, let's consider this analogy and answer choices:

> warm : hot :: _____ : hilarious
> **a.** humid
> **b.** raucous
> **c.** summer
> **d.** amusing

To come up with the correct answer, you must first figure out the relationship. This is an analogy of degrees. Warm is less intense than hot, therefore what answer choice is something that is less intense than hilarious? The right answer is **d**, based on the relationship of amusing being less intense than hilarious. To illustrate how some test takers get led astray by carefully crafted wrong answer choices, let's take a closer look at choices **a**, **b**, and **c**. Some test takers will impulsively pick **a** because humid is related to the first word pair, warm and hot, but it is not part of the analogy of degree. This choice is offered as an option for the careless reader. Other test takers will choose **b** because they have misunderstood the analogy. They may think that the word pair, warm : hot, is a synonym pair, showing faulty reasoning skills. Choosing **c** is a slightly different case. Wrong answers may also be chosen because of the test taker's predisposition. In this example, summer is chosen because warm : hot reminds the test taker of summer. These are all illustrations of ways in which test takers can get thrown off or distracted by wrong answer choices. Careful, close reading, and lots of practice will help you to avoid the wrong answer trap. And remember, as time runs out, you are more prone to make careless mistakes, so read carefully and stay calm. Your reasoning skills and power of logic work better when you are not flustered, so remain in control and stay alert.

Finally, let's tackle the time issue. Most assessment tests are timed, and time can be an important factor with analogy questions. Most test takers have the necessary knowledge to answer the majority of analogy questions, what many test takers don't have is the ability to answer the questions quickly. As you become more familiar with analogy questions, you will find that you can answer the questions more quickly. You will be able to move through the basic questions with confidence and allow yourself more time with the advanced questions without feeling the pressure of the clock.

Each chapter contains between 35 and 50 questions, and the correct answers are explained at the end of each chapter. The answer section provides you with not only the right answer, but also the relationship that is used to solve the analogy. Use your performance to create a study guide. For example, examine your answers to determine if a particular type of analogy question is giving you trouble. You may also find that your lack of word knowledge is causing you to answer questions incorrectly. In this case you can spend time studying word lists to improve your performance. If you are simply having trouble with the more difficult questions, then more practice is the answer. If you are looking for more challenging analogies, Chapter 12 is made up of more difficult analogy questions. In addition, if you are studying for the Miller Analogies Test (MAT), don't miss Chapter 13, which contains analogies that are great practice for this unique test.

You have already taken an important step toward improving your score. You have shown your commitment by purchasing this book. Now all you need to do is complete each exercise, study the answers, and watch your ability to solve analogies increase. You can even work in pencil and do the exercises again to reinforce what you have learned. Good luck!

# 1

## Word Analogy Practice

**1.** _____ : trail :: grain : grail
  **a.** train
  **b.** path
  **c.** wheat
  **d.** holy

**2.** particular : fussy ::
  _____ : subservient
  **a.** meek
  **b.** above
  **c.** cranky
  **d.** uptight

**3.** _____ : horse ::
  board : train
  **a.** stable
  **b.** shoe
  **c.** ride
  **d.** mount

**4.** tureen : _____ ::
  goblet : wine
  **a.** napkin
  **b.** soup
  **c.** spoon
  **d.** pilsner

**5.** 4 : 6 :: _____ : 16
  **a.** 2
  **b.** 14
  **c.** 8
  **d.** 10

**6.** son : nuclear ::
  _____ : extended
  **a.** father
  **b.** mother
  **c.** cousin
  **d.** daughters

**7.** coif : hair :: _____ : musical
   **a.** shower
   **b.** close
   **c.** praise
   **d.** score

**8.** feta : Greek ::
   provolone : _____
   **a.** salad
   **b.** Swiss
   **c.** blue
   **d.** Italian

**9.** moccasin : snake ::
   _____ : shoe
   **a.** alligator
   **b.** waders
   **c.** asp
   **d.** loafer

**10.** _____ : zenith ::
   fear : composure
   **a.** apex
   **b.** heaven
   **c.** heights
   **d.** nadir

**11.** pill : bore :: core : _____
   **a.** center
   **b.** mug
   **c.** bar
   **d.** placebo

**12.** pilfer : steal :: _____ : equip
   **a.** return
   **b.** damage
   **c.** exercise
   **d.** furnish

**13.** native : aboriginal ::
   naïve : _____
   **a.** learned
   **b.** arid
   **c.** unsophisticated
   **d.** tribe

**14.** junket : _____ :: junk : trash
   **a.** trounce
   **b.** trip
   **c.** refuse
   **d.** trinket

**15.** _____ : festive ::
   funeral : somber
   **a.** tension
   **b.** soiree
   **c.** eulogy
   **d.** sari

**16.** fetish : fixation ::
   slight : _____
   **a.** flirt
   **b.** sloth
   **c.** insult
   **d.** confuse

**17.** hovel : dirty :: hub : _____
   **a.** unseen
   **b.** prideful
   **c.** busy
   **d.** shovel

**18.** bog : _____ ::
   slumber : sleep
   **a.** dream
   **b.** foray
   **c.** marsh
   **d.** night

**19.** _____ : segue ::
throng : mass
**a.** subway
**b.** church
**c.** transition
**d.** line

**20.** ragtime : United States ::
raga : _____
**a.** cloth
**b.** country
**c.** piano
**d.** India

**21.** miserly : cheap ::
homogeneous : _____
**a.** extravagant
**b.** unkind
**c.** alike
**d.** friendly

**22.** skew : gloomy ::
slant : _____
**a.** glee
**b.** foible
**c.** desperate
**d.** gloaming

**23.** eider : _____ :: cedar : tree
**a.** snow
**b.** plant
**c.** duck
**d.** pine

**24.** gerrymander : divide ::
filibuster : _____
**a.** bend
**b.** punish
**c.** delay
**d.** rush

**25.** vapid : _____ :: rapid : swift
**a.** inspired
**b.** turgid
**c.** wet
**d.** insipid

**26.** denim : cotton ::
_____ : flax
**a.** sheep
**b.** uniform
**c.** sweater
**d.** linen

**27.** obscene : coarse ::
obtuse : _____
**a.** subject
**b.** obstinate
**c.** obscure
**d.** stupid

**28.** diamond : baseball ::
court : _____
**a.** poker
**b.** jury
**c.** grass
**d.** squash

**29.** quixotic : pragmatic ::
murky : _____
a. rapid
b. cloudy
c. clear
d. friendly

**30.** smear : libel :: heed : _____
a. represent
b. doubt
c. consider
d. need

**31.** nymph : _____ ::
seraphim : angel
a. maiden
b. sinner
c. candle
d. priest

**32.** poetry : rhyme ::
philosophy : _____
a. imagery
b. music
c. bi-law
d. theory

**33.** jibe : praise ::
_____ : enlighten
a. jib
b. delude
c. worship
d. wed

**34.** marshal : prisoner ::
principal : _____
a. teacher
b. president
c. doctrine
d. student

**35.** fecund : infertile ::
_____ : fleet
a. rapid
b. slow
c. fertilizer
d. damp

# Answers

**1. a. Train** becomes trail when the "n" is replaced by an "l," and grain becomes grail when the "n" is replaced by an "l."

**2. a.** Particular is a synonym for fussy, and **meek** is a synonym for subservient.

**3. d.** To **mount** means to get on a horse, and to board means to get on a train.

**4. b.** A tureen is used to hold **soup**, and a goblet is used to hold wine.

**5. b.** 4 plus 2 is 6, and **14** plus 2 is 16.

**6. c.** A son is part of a nuclear family, and a **cousin** is part of an extended family.

**7. d.** To coif means to arrange hair, and to **score** means to arrange a musical.

**8. d.** Feta is a Greek cheese, and provolone is an **Italian** cheese.

**9. d.** A moccasin is a type of snake, and a **loafer** is a type of shoe.

**10. d. Nadir** is the opposite of zenith, and fear is the opposite of composure.

**11. a.** A pill is another word for a bore, and a core is another word for a **center**.

**12. d.** To pilfer means to steal, and to **furnish** means to equip.

**13. c.** Native is a synonym for aboriginal, and naïve is a synonym for **unsophisticated**.

**14. b.** A junket is a synonym for a **trip**, and junk is a synonym for trash.

**15.** **b.** A **soiree** is described as festive, and a funeral is described as somber.

**16.** **c.** A fetish is a synonym for a fixation, and a slight is a synonym for an **insult**.

**17.** **c.** A hovel is described as dirty, and a hub is described as **busy**.

**18.** **c.** A bog is a synonym for a **marsh**, and slumber is a synonym for sleep.

**19.** **c.** A **transition** is a synonym for a segue, and a throng is a synonym for a mass.

**20.** **d.** Ragtime is a type of music from the United States, and raga is a type of music from **India**.

**21.** **c.** Miserly is another word for cheap, and homogeneous is another word for **alike**.

**22.** **c.** To skew is a synonym of to slant, and to be gloomy is a synonym for **desperate**.

**23.** **c.** An eider is a type of **duck**, and a cedar is a type of tree.

**24.** **c.** To gerrymander is a political term meaning to divide land, and to filibuster is to **delay** legislature.

**25.** **d.** Vapid is another word for **insipid**, and rapid is another word for swift.

**26.** **d.** Denim is a fabric made from cotton, and **linen** is a fabric made from flax.

**27.** **d.** Obscene is a synonym for coarse, and obtuse is a synonym for **stupid**.

**28.** **d.** Baseball is played on a diamond, and **squash** is played on a court.

**29. c.** Quixotic is an antonym for pragmatic, and murky is an antonym for **clear**.

**30. c.** To smear is a synonym of to libel, and to heed is a synonym of to **consider**.

**31. a.** A nymph is a **maiden**, and a seraphim is an angel.

**32. d.** Poetry is often comprised of rhyme; philosophy is often built on **theory**.

**33. b.** To jibe is an antonym of to praise, and to **delude** is an antonym of to enlighten.

**34. d.** A marshal is a person in charge of a prisoner, and a principal is a person in charge of a **student**.

**35. b.** Fecund is an antonym for infertile, and **slow** is an antonym for fleet.

# 2

# Word Analogy Practice

**36.** mend : sewing ::
edit : _____
a. darn
b. repair
c. manuscript
d. makeshift

**37.** abet : _____ :: alone : lone
a. bet
b. loan
c. wager
d. single

**38.** 80 : 40 :: 2 : _____
a. 8
b. 4
c. 1
d. 20

**39.** piercing : _____ ::
hushed : whisper
a. diamond
b. watch
c. siren
d. ears

**40.** segregate : unify ::
repair : _____
a. approach
b. push
c. damage
d. outwit

**41.** congeal : solidify ::
_____ : char
a. conceal
b. singe
c. evaporate
d. charge

**42.** _____ : marsupial ::
monkey : primate
a. opossum
b. ape
c. honeybee
d. moose

**43.** principle : doctrine ::
living : _____
a. will
b. dead
c. likelihood
d. livelihood

**44.** _____ : climb ::
recession : withdrawal
a. ascent
b. absence
c. dollar
d. absorption

**45.** myopic : farsighted ::
_____ : obscure
a. benevolent
b. famous
c. turgid
d. wasted

**46.** shallot : _____ ::
scallop : mollusk
a. shark
b. muscle
c. dessert
d. onion

**47.** conjugate : pair ::
partition : _____
a. divide
b. consecrate
c. parade
d. squelch

**48.** _____ : excerpt ::
exercise : maneuver
a. exception
b. passage
c. routine
d. cause

**49.** alphabetical : _____ ::
sequential : files
a. sort
b. part
c. list
d. order

**50.** tacit : implied ::
_____ : inferior
a. shoddy
b. taciturn
c. forthright
d. superior

**51.** implement : rule ::
_____ : verdict
a. propose
b. render
c. divide
d. teach

**52.** vaunt : boast ::
skewer : _____
  **a.** flaunt
  **b.** criticize
  **c.** prepare
  **d.** avoid

**53.** gambol : _____ ::
gamble : bet
  **a.** skip
  **b.** win
  **c.** bat
  **d.** worship

**54.** rotation : earth ::
_____ : top
  **a.** planet
  **b.** spinning
  **c.** sun
  **d.** expanding

**55.** gall : vex :: hex : _____
  **a.** fix
  **b.** jinx
  **c.** index
  **d.** vixen

**56.** monarch : _____ ::
king : cobra
  **a.** queen
  **b.** butterfly
  **c.** royal
  **d.** venom

**57.** iota : jot :: _____ : type
  **a.** one
  **b.** ilk
  **c.** tab
  **d.** jet

**58.** _____ : subject :: veer : path
  **a.** object
  **b.** prove
  **c.** math
  **d.** digress

**59.** pan : _____ :: ban : judge
  **a.** band
  **b.** critic
  **c.** author
  **d.** lawyer

**60.** _____ : oyster :: paddy : rice
  **a.** aphrodisiac
  **b.** mollusk
  **c.** bed
  **d.** sandwich

**61.** cicada : _____ ::
collie : canine
  **a.** fruit
  **b.** mineral
  **c.** cat
  **d.** insect

**62.** huckster : _____ ::
gangster : crime
  **a.** corn
  **b.** trucking
  **c.** policeman
  **d.** advertising

**63.** _____ : bedrock ::
cement : foundation
  **a.** mica
  **b.** water
  **c.** lava
  **d.** sand

**64.** dolorous : _____ ::
sonorous : loud
a. woozy
b. weepy
c. dull
d. sleepy

**65.** lapidary : _____ ::
dramaturge : plays
a. cows
b. gems
c. rabbits
d. movies

**66.** penurious : _____ ::
deep : significant
a. generous
b. stingy
c. decrepit
d. cavernous

**67.** somnolent : nap ::
truculent : _____
a. sleepwalker
b. journey
c. war
d. mood

**68.** nictitate : _____ ::
expectorate : spit
a. wink
b. stomp
c. quit
d. smoke

**69.** cytology : _____ ::
geology : rocks
a. cyclones
b. psychology
c. pharmacology
d. cells

**70.** proboscis : _____ ::
abdomen : gut
a. prognosis
b. nose
c. ear
d. nausea

# Answers

**36.** **c.** One fixes sewing by mending; one fixes **manuscript** by editing.

**37.** **a.** Abet becomes **bet** when the "a" is removed, and alone becomes lone when the "a" is removed.

**38.** **c.** Half of 80 is 40, and half of 2 is **1**.

**39.** **c.** A **siren** is described as piercing, and a whisper is described as hushed.

**40.** **c.** To segregate is an antonym of to unify, and to repair is an antonym of to **damage**.

**41.** **b.** To congeal means to solidify, and to **singe** means to char.

**42.** **a.** A monkey is an example of a primate, and an **opossum** is an example of a marsupial.

**43.** **d.** A principle is another word for a doctrine, and a living is another word for **livelihood**.

**44.** **a.** An **ascent** is a climb, and a recession is a withdrawal.

**45.** **b.** Myopic is an antonym for farsighted, and **famous** is an antonym of obscure.

**46.** **d.** A shallot is a type of **onion**, and a scallop is a type of mollusk.

**47.** **a.** To conjugate means to pair, and to partition means to **divide**.

**48.** **b.** A **passage** is another word for an excerpt, and an exercise is another word for a maneuver.

**49.** **c.** Alphabetical describes the ordering of a **list**, and sequential describes the ordering of files.

**50. a.** Tacit is another word for implied, and **shoddy** is another word for inferior.

**51. b.** A rule is implemented, and a verdict is **rendered**.

**52. b.** To vaunt means to boast, and to skewer means to **criticize**.

**53. a.** To gambol means to **skip**, and to gamble means to bet.

**54. b.** Rotation is the movement of the earth and **spinning** is the movement of a top.

**55. b.** To gall is to vex, and to hex is to **jinx**.

**56. b.** A monarch is a type of **butterfly** and a king is a type of cobra.

**57. b.** Iota and jot are synonyms, as are **ilk** and type.

**58. d.** One **digresses** from a subject, and one veers from a path.

**59. b.** Pan is something a **critic** does, and ban is something a judge does.

**60. c.** Oysters grow in a **bed** of the ocean, and rice grows in a paddy.

**61. d.** A cicada is a type of **insect**, and a collie is a type of canine.

**62. d.** A huckster is one who deals in **advertising**, and a gangster is one who deals in crime.

**63. a.** **Mica** makes up bedrock—on which skyscrapers are built; cement makes up a foundation—on which houses are built.

**64. b.** Dolorous is a synonym for **weepy**, and sonorous is a synonym for loud.

**65. b.** A lapidary is one who works with **gems**, and a dramaturge works with plays.

**66.** **b.** Penurious is a synonym for **stingy**, and deep is a synonym for significant.

**67.** **c.** Being somnolent can lead to a nap, and being truculent can lead to **war**.

**68.** **a.** To nictitate means to **wink**, and to expectorate means to spit.

**69.** **d.** Cytology is the study of **cells**, and geology is the study of rocks.

**70.** **b.** Proboscis means **nose**, and abdomen means gut.

# 3

## Word Analogy Practice

**71.** rein : horse ::
control panel : _____
a. pilot
b. bit
c. plane
d. rider

**72.** Argentina : Brazil ::
_____ : Iran
a. Canada
b. Iraq
c. Ireland
d. Mexico

**73.** _____ : play :: sing : anthem
a. act
b. scene
c. theater
d. field

**74.** mouse : _____ ::
flash : camera
a. rat
b. computer
c. cord
d. dessert

**75.** cushion : sofa ::
shelf : _____
a. ledge
b. bookcase
c. storage
d. frame

**76.** scrub : wash :: sob : _____
a. cry
b. water
c. sad
d. tease

**77.** moisten : _____ ::
cool : freeze
a. water
b. soak
c. oven
d. grow

**78.** persimmon : _____ ::
cottontail : rabbit
a. cinnamon
b. oven
c. badger
d. berry

**79.** stars : astronomy ::
_____ : history
a. battles
b. eclipse
c. horse
d. autumn

**80.** _____ : unity ::
dearth : scarcity
a. belief
b. death
c. cohesion
d. fear

**81.** Aesop : fable ::
Homer : _____
a. temple
b. donkey
c. epic
d. Greece

**82.** turncoat : traitor ::
_____ : rogue
a. scamp
b. pillow
c. blush
d. tricky

**83.** hanker : _____ ::
ponder : think
a. junk
b. fool
c. yearn
d. bunker

**84.** rook : chess ::
_____ : badminton
a. grass
b. tennis
c. shuttlecock
d. swing

**85.** bowler : _____ ::
satchel : bag
a. hat
b. lane
c. trophy
d. ottoman

**86.** _____ : wood :: file : nail
a. hammer
b. cabinet
c. saw
d. plane

**87.** volume : _____ ::
stanza : poem
a. measure
b. pint
c. encyclopedia
d. kitchen

**88.** _____ : dolphin ::
herd : cow
a. ocean
b. pod
c. porpoise
d. leap

**89.** pharaoh : dynasty ::
_____ : democracy
a. government
b. election
c. president
d. Canada

**90.** deplete : decrease ::
_____ : avoid
a. danger
b. dislike
c. miss
d. shun

**91.** chatter : talk ::
flutter : _____
a. dance
b. wobble
c. sing
d. flap

**92.** plead : _____ ::
submerge : dip
a. avoid
b. dismiss
c. ask
d. covet

**93.** doze : sleep :: tiptoe : _____
a. walk
b. flat
c. shelf
d. swim

**94.** ledger : accounts ::
_____ : observations
a. pundit
b. weather
c. astrology
d. diary

**95.** _____ : money :: urn : ashes
a. cash
b. wealth
c. purse
d. inheritance

**96.** egregious : bad ::
_____ : small
a. minuscule
b. tall
c. wicked
d. cheap

**97.** approach : _____ ::
leave : bolt
a. pounce
b. arrive
c. demand
d. airport

**98.** lawless : order ::
captive : _____
a. trouble
b. punishment
c. jail
d. freedom

**99.** quarry : marble ::
_____ : honey
a. hive
b. bee
c. spread
d. reservoir

**100.** seemly : _____ ::
torrid : scorching
a. burnt
b. invisible
c. attractive
d. horrid

**101.** bivouac : _____ ::
axis : alliance
a. diplomacy
b. sergeant
c. soldier
d. camp

**102.** pineapple : _____ ::
orange : Florida
a. Dole
b. Hawaii
c. Canada
d. mango

**103.** quicksilver : mercury ::
goldbrick : _____
a. worker
b. idler
c. money
d. idol

**104.** ribbon : _____ ::
icing : cake
a. present
b. cut
c. bow
d. typewriter

**105.** search : _____ ::
defeat : vanquish
a. peer
b. ransack
c. destroy
d. find

# Answers

**71.** **c.** A rider uses a rein to guide a horse; a pilot uses the control panel to guide a **plane**.

**72.** **b.** The country of Argentina neighbors the country of Brazil. Similarly, **Iraq** borders Iran.

**73.** **a.** One **acts** in a play, and one sings an anthem.

**74.** **b.** A mouse is part of a **computer**, and a flash is a part of a camera.

**75.** **b.** A cushion is a part of a sofa, and a shelf is part of a **bookcase**.

**76.** **a.** To scrub is to wash vigorously, and to sob is to **cry** convulsively.

**77.** **b.** To moisten is to wet less intensely than to **soak**, and to cool is to reduce the temperature less intensely than to freeze.

**78.** **d.** A persimmon is a type of **berry**, and a cottontail is a type of rabbit.

**79.** **a.** Stars are a component of astronomy, and **battles** make up history.

**80.** **c.** **Cohesion** and unity are synonyms, as are dearth and scarcity.

**81.** **c.** Aesop is known for writing fables, and Homer is known for writing **epics**.

**82.** **a.** Turncoat is another word for traitor, and **scamp** is another word for rogue.

**83.** **c.** Hanker is another word for **yearn**, and ponder is another word for think.

**84.** **c.** A rook is a piece used in the game of chess, and a **shuttlecock** is used to play the game of badminton.

**85.** **a.** A bowler is a type of **hat**, and a satchel is a type of bag.

**86.** **d.** A **plane** is a tool used to smooth and shape wood, and a file is a tool used to smooth and shape a nail.

**87.** **c.** A volume is part of an **encyclopedia**, and a stanza is part of a poem.

**88.** **b.** A **pod** is a group of dolphins, and a herd is a group of cows.

**89.** **c.** A pharaoh is the head of a dynasty, or ruling family, and a **president** is the head of a democracy.

**90.** **d.** To deplete is to decrease completely, and to **shun** is to avoid completely.

**91.** **d.** To chatter is to talk rapidly, and to flutter is to **flap** rapidly.

**92.** **c.** To plead is to **ask** urgently, and to submerge is to dip completely.

**93.** **a.** To doze is to sleep lightly, and to tiptoe is to **walk** lightly.

**94.** **d.** A ledger is a book that contains accounts, and a **diary** is a book that contains observations.

**95.** **c.** A **purse** is used to hold money, and an urn is used to hold ashes.

**96.** **a.** Egregious means very bad, and **minuscule** means very small.

**97.** **a.** To **pounce** is to approach suddenly, and to bolt is to leave suddenly.

**98.** **d.** To be lawless is to lack order, and to be captive is to lack **freedom**.

**99.** **a.** A quarry yields marble, and a **hive** yields honey.

**100. c.** Seemly is a synonym for **attractive**, and torrid is a synonym for scorching.

**101. d.** A bivouac is another word for a **camp**, and an axis is another word for an alliance.

**102. b.** Pineapples are grown in **Hawaii**, and oranges are grown in Florida.

**103. b.** Quicksilver is a synonym for mercury, and goldbrick is a synonym for an **idler**.

**104. a.** A ribbon is used to decorate a **present**, and icing is used to decorate a cake.

**105. b.** To **ransack** is to search thoroughly, and to vanquish is defeat thoroughly.

# Word Analogy Practice

**106.** kitten : _____ ::
soldier : army
**a.** cat
**b.** litter
**c.** puppy
**d.** meow

**107.** cord : telephone ::
_____ : television
**a.** watch
**b.** screen
**c.** program
**d.** table

**108.** cub : bear :: joey : _____
**a.** cave
**b.** doll
**c.** kangaroo
**d.** truck

**109.** fern : plant :: _____ : fish
**a.** catch
**b.** minnow
**c.** animal
**d.** sparrow

**110.** _____ : wrist :: belt : waist
**a.** arm
**b.** hand
**c.** bend
**d.** bracelet

**111.** shark : _____ :: slug : land
**a.** seaweed
**b.** ocean
**c.** sky
**d.** slide

**112.** hangar : airplane ::
garage : _____
a. steak
b. runway
c. oil
d. automobile

**113.** ramp : highway ::
_____ : house
a. traffic
b. head
c. door
d. speed

**114.** hint : _____ ::
whisper : shout
a. demand
b. point
c. surprise
d. secret

**115.** dog : kennel :: bird : _____
a. fly
b. feather
c. aerie
d. eagle

**116.** _____ : codes ::
ornithology : birds
a. cartography
b. husbandry
c. species
d. cryptography

**117.** _____ : poem :: fable : story
a. epic
b. poet
c. haiku
d. rhyme

**118.** jetty : _____ ::
bouquet : flowers
a. daffodils
b. beach
c. rocks
d. water

**119.** spoke : _____ ::
word : sentence
a. speaker
b. paragraph
c. comma
d. wheel

**120.** secret : furtive ::
audible : _____
a. resonant
b. nap
c. sack
d. ring

**121.** vamp : shoe :: hood : _____
a. jacket
b. car
c. clean
d. crook

**122.** fleet : trucks ::
_____ : teachers
a. apple
b. student
c. book
d. faculty

**123.** _____ : assistant ::
administrator : teacher
a. office
b. school
c. executive
d. campus

**124.** algebra : calculus ::
_____ : surgery
a. anatomy
b. knife
c. doctor
d. hospital

**125.** pride : _____ :: calm : storm
a. proud
b. forecast
c. sunny
d. fall

**126.** _____ : clue :: pig : truffle
a. detective
b. hog
c. chocolate
d. France

**127.** scientist : experiment ::
_____ : play
a. beaker
b. rehearsal
c. actor
d. lab

**128.** sloth : action ::
_____ : principles
a. unscrupulousness
b. teachers
c. hero
d. conscientious

**129.** _____ : speak :: roam : walk
a. path
b. silent
c. write
d. babble

**130.** epilogue : novel ::
_____ : meal
a. dessert
b. repast
c. lunch
d. appetizer

**131.** _____ : tennis :: drive : golf
a. net
b. score
c. racket
d. serve

**132.** _____ : court case ::
abstract : research paper
a. brief
b. judge
c. hypothesis
d. lawyer

**133.** _____ : peace ::
lion : courage
a. war
b. brave
c. dove
d. cub

**134.** tooth : _____ :: tine : fork
a. molar
b. tongue
c. comb
d. spoon

**135.** grove : forest :: _____ : lake
   **a.** pond
   **b.** ocean
   **c.** tree
   **d.** boat

**136.** trot : _____ :: jog : sprint
   **a.** drive
   **b.** canter
   **c.** horse
   **d.** speed

**137.** shower : deluge ::
_____ : stare
   **a.** wet
   **b.** window
   **c.** ignore
   **d.** glance

**138.** _____ : mug ::
trowel : spade
   **a.** coffee
   **b.** dig
   **c.** tumbler
   **d.** tavern

**139.** carousel : luggage ::
escalator : _____
   **a.** raise
   **b.** elevator
   **c.** people
   **d.** building

**140.** irrelevant : significance ::
relaxed : _____
   **a.** care
   **b.** calm
   **c.** thoughtful
   **d.** asleep

**141.** pummel : hit ::
_____ : recite
   **a.** disbelief
   **b.** poem
   **c.** chant
   **d.** question

**142.** gobble : eat ::
_____ : accept
   **a.** deny
   **b.** embrace
   **c.** acquiesce
   **d.** infer

**143.** company : conglomerate ::
metal : _____
   **a.** alloy
   **b.** aluminum
   **c.** corporation
   **d.** furnace

**144.** _____ : silo :: art : museum
   **a.** field
   **b.** fodder
   **c.** farm
   **d.** windmill

**145.** _____ : grind :: ax : chop
   **a.** tree
   **b.** coffee
   **c.** pestle
   **d.** saw

# Answers

**106. b.** A kitten is part of a **litter**, and a soldier is part of an army.

**107. b.** A cord of part of a telephone, and a **screen** is part of a television.

**108. c.** A cub is a young bear, and a joey is a young **kangaroo**.

**109. b.** A fern is a type of plant, and a **minnow** is a type of fish.

**110. d.** A **bracelet** is worn around the wrist, and a belt is worn around the waist.

**111. b.** A shark lives in the **ocean**, and a slug lives on land.

**112. d.** A hangar houses an airplane, and a garage houses an **automobile**.

**113. c.** You enter and exit a highway by a ramp and you enter and exit a house by a **door**.

**114. a.** To hint is to ask subtly and to **demand** is to ask insistently, and whisper is to talk quietly and to shout is to talk loudly.

**115. c.** A kennel houses dogs, and an **aerie** houses birds.

**116. d. Cryptography** is the study of codes, and ornithology is the study of birds.

**117. c.** A **haiku** is a type of poem, and a fable is a type of story.

**118. c.** A jetty is composed of **rocks**, and a bouquet is composed of flowers.

**119. d.** A spoke is part of a **wheel**, and a word is part of a sentence.

**120. a.** Furtive is more intensely secret, and **resonant** is more intensely audible.

**121.** **b.** A vamp is part of a shoe, and a hood is part of a **car**.

**122.** **d.** A fleet is a group of trucks, and a **faculty** is a group of teachers.

**123.** **c.** An **executive** manages an assistant, and an administrator manages a teacher.

**124.** **a.** Algebra is a prerequisite for calculus, and **anatomy** is a prerequisite for surgery.

**125.** **d.** According to two well-known expressions, pride comes before a **fall**, and calm comes before the storm.

**126.** **a.** A **detective** hunts for clues, and a pig hunts for truffles.

**127.** **c.** A scientist performs an experiment, and an **actor** performs a play.

**128.** **a.** Sloth is a lack of action, and **unscrupulousness** is a lack of principles.

**129.** **d.** **Babble** is a way to speak, and roam is a way to walk.

**130.** **a.** An epilogue comes at the end of a novel, and a **dessert** comes at the end of a meal.

**131.** **d.** A **serve** is an action in tennis, and a drive is an action in golf.

**132.** **a.** A **brief** is a summary of a court case, and an abstract is a summary of a research paper.

**133.** **c.** A **dove** is a symbol of peace, and a lion is a symbol of courage.

**134.** **c.** A tooth is part of a **comb**, and a tine is part of a fork.

**135.** **a.** A grove is a smaller version of a forest, and a **pond** is a smaller version of a lake.

**136.** **b.** To trot is slower than to **canter**, and to jog is slower than to sprint.

**137.** **d.** A shower is a less intense version of a deluge, and a **glance** is a less intense version of a stare.

**138.** **c.** Both a **tumbler** and a mug are used as drinking vessels, and a trowel and a spade are used as garden tools.

**139.** **c.** A carousel is used to move luggage, and an escalator is used to move **people**.

**140.** **a.** To be irrelevant is to lack significance, and to be relaxed is to be free of **care**.

**141.** **c.** To pummel is to hit repeatedly, and to **chant** is to recite repeatedly.

**142.** **b.** To gobble is to eat to eagerly, and to **embrace** is to accept readily.

**143.** **a.** A company is part of a conglomerate, and a metal is part of an **alloy**.

**144.** **b.** **Fodder** is kept in a silo, and art is kept in a museum.

**145.** **c.** A **pestle** is a tool for grinding, and an ax is a tool for chopping.

# 5

# Word Analogy Practice

**146.** _____ : highway ::
net : court
**a.** road
**b.** radar
**c.** ticket
**d.** median

**147.** crumb : bread ::
_____ : molecule
**a.** shard
**b.** atom
**c.** trail
**d.** ion

**148.** _____ : launch ::
breakfast : lunch
**a.** sandwich
**b.** dinner
**c.** eggs
**d.** countdown

**149.** churn : _____ :: press : wine
**a.** paddle
**b.** cream
**c.** butter
**d.** stomach

**150.** collar : shirt :: _____ : hat
**a.** button
**b.** visor
**c.** pullover
**d.** hood

**151.** dough : bread ::
_____ : pancake
**a.** griddle
**b.** cake
**c.** batter
**d.** oven

**152.** _____ : skid ::
obstacle : swerve
a. bike
b. ice
c. wheel
d. roadway

**153.** wheat : chaff ::
quality : _____
a. thresh
b. whole
c. inadequacy
d. worth

**154.** _____ : forgiveness ::
bribe : influence
a. quarrel
b. lie
c. apology
d. perjury

**155.** follow : chase ::
nudge : _____
a. thrust
b. pursue
c. catch
d. precede

**156.** cancel : delay ::
surrender : _____
a. anticipate
b. yield
c. fire
d. army

**157.** holster : pistol ::
_____ : knife
a. weapon
b. rifle
c. sheath
d. club

**158.** thicket : shrubs ::
_____ : stars
a. sun
b. cluster
c. orbit
d. moon

**159.** postmortem : _____ ::
rainbow : downpour
a. address
b. forecast
c. morning
d. death

**160.** rake : leaves ::
_____ : information
a. homeowner
b. profile
c. census
d. lawn

**161.** _____ : tradition ::
hedonist : pleasure
a. purist
b. Eden
c. displeasure
d. agnostic

**162.** swing : ax :: _____ : sword
  **a.** honor
  **b.** dull
  **c.** parry
  **d.** knife

**163.** elevator : transport ::
rickshaw : _____
  **a.** train
  **b.** bicycle
  **c.** carry
  **d.** slip-shod

**164.** lightweight : _____ ::
sedan : automobile
  **a.** beam
  **b.** boxer
  **c.** heavyweight
  **d.** traffic

**165.** knave : _____ ::
coward : bravery
  **a.** retreat
  **b.** beauty
  **c.** truth
  **d.** stoicism

**166.** _____ : ship ::
telescope : star
  **a.** deck
  **b.** water
  **c.** periscope
  **d.** astronomy

**167.** tarpaulin : rain ::
_____ : stain
  **a.** stove
  **b.** picnic
  **c.** puddle
  **d.** apron

**168.** sniff : inhale :: _____ : lop
  **a.** crush
  **b.** snit
  **c.** snip
  **d.** adhere

**169.** outrage : peeve ::
strive : _____
  **a.** attempt
  **b.** curse
  **c.** duel
  **d.** shun

**170.** decrescendo : _____ ::
recession : economy
  **a.** crescendo
  **b.** finance
  **c.** boom
  **d.** volume

**171.** thrifty : _____ ::
hungry : gluttonous
  **a.** virtue
  **b.** vice
  **c.** avarice
  **d.** self-control

**172.** privy : secret ::
sympathetic : _____
a. spy
b. grief
c. clandestine
d. joy

**173.** pallid : color ::
tactless : _____
a. hue
b. tasteless
c. verve
d. diplomatic

**174.** din : _____ :: odor : garbage
a. crowd
b. tree
c. dark
d. nose

**175.** _____ : incising ::
spatula : lifting
a. pancake
b. bullhorn
c. scalpel
d. truck

**176.** break : shift ::
minute : _____
a. second
b. hour
c. spell
d. work

**177.** _____ : service :: juror : jury
a. inductee
b. judge
c. martial
d. sequester

**178.** ratchet : _____ ::
grow : inches
a. tools
b. shrink
c. yards
d. stages

**179.** cellar : house :: _____ : ship
a. land
b. hold
c. ocean
d. wave

**180.** economy : parsimony ::
_____ : rift
a. disagreement
b. fissure
c. bounty
d. river

**181.** admonish : _____ ::
defeat : conquer
a. administer
b. celebrate
c. negotiate
d. berate

**182.** _____ : wheat ::
lentil : legume
a. barley
b. bread
c. soup
d. spelt

**183.** mercenary : wages ::
dilettante : _____
a. enjoyment
b. rifle
c. strife
d. market

**184.** candle : illuminate ::
_____ : cool
a. breeze
b. wick
c. burn
d. refrigerator

**185.** fop : _____ ::
documentary : reality
a. appearance
b. movie
c. punishment
d. fairytale

## Answers

**146.** **d.** A **median** divides a highway, and a net divides a court, as in tennis.

**147.** **b.** A crumb is a particle of bread, and an **atom** is a particle of a molecule.

**148.** **d.** A **countdown** precedes a launch, and breakfast precedes lunch.

**149.** **c.** A churn is used to make **butter**, and a press is used to make wine.

**150.** **b.** A collar is part of a shirt, and a **visor** is part of a hat.

**151.** **c.** Dough becomes bread in the cooking process, and **batter** becomes a pancake.

**152.** **b.** **Ice** can cause something to skid, and an obstacle can cause something to swerve.

**153.** **c.** Wheat is an antonym of chaff, and quality is an antonym of **inadequacy**.

**154.** **c.** An **apology** is used to attain forgiveness, and a bribe is used to attain influence.

**155.** **a.** To follow is less intense than to chase, and to nudge is less intense than to **thrust**.

**156.** **b.** To cancel is more intense than to delay, and to surrender is more intense than to **yield**.

**157.** **c.** A holster holds a pistol, and a **sheath** holds a knife.

**158.** **b.** A thicket is a group of shrubs, and a **cluster** is a group of stars.

**159.** **d.** A postmortem follows a **death**, and a rainbow occurs after a downpour.

**160.** **c.** A rake is used to gather grass, and a **census** is used to gather information.

**161.** **a.** A **purist** is fixated on tradition, and a hedonist is fixated on pleasure.

**162.** **c.** Swing is an action taken with an ax, and **parry** is an action taken with a sword.

**163.** **c.** An elevator is used to transport people, and a rickshaw is used to **carry** people.

**164.** **b.** Lightweight is a classification for a **boxer**, and sedan is a classification for an automobile.

**165.** **c.** A knave is one who does not exhibit the **truth**, and a coward does not exhibit bravery.

**166.** **c.** A **periscope** is used to look for ships, and a telescope is used to look for stars.

**167.** **d.** A tarpaulin is used to protect from rain, and an **apron** is used to protect from stains.

**168.** **c.** To sniff is less intense than to inhale, and to **snip** is less intense than to lop.

**169.** **a.** To outrage is more intense than to peeve, and to strive is more intense than to **attempt**.

**170.** **d.** A decrescendo is a reduction in **volume**, and a recession is a reduction in the economy.

**171.** **c.** Thrifty describes **avarice**, and hungry describes gluttonous.

**172.** **b.** Privy is sharing in a secret, and sympathetic is sharing in **grief**.

**173.** **d.** Pallid means lacking in color, and tactless means lacking **diplomacy**.

**174.** **a.** Din, or noise, is a word associated with a **crowd**, and odor is a word associated with garbage.

**175.** **c.** A **scalpel** is used to make an incision, and a spatula is used for lifting.

**176.** **b.** A break is part of a shift, and a minute is part of an **hour**.

**177.** **a.** An **inductee** is a person in military service, and a juror is a member of a jury.

**178.** **d.** To ratchet means to increase by **stages**, and to grow is to increase by inches.

**179.** **b.** A cellar is a lower storage area in a house, and a **hold** is a lower storage area on a ship.

**180.** **b.** Economy is a synonym of parsimony, and **fissure** is a synonym of rift.

**181.** **d.** To admonish is less intense than to **berate**, and to defeat is less intense than to conquer.

**182.** **d.** **Spelt** is a type of wheat, and lentil is a type of legume.

**183.** **a.** A mercenary performs a task for wages, and a dilettante does something for **enjoyment**.

**184.** **d.** A candle illuminates when in use; a **refrigerator** cools when in use.

**185.** **a.** A fop is concerned with **appearance**, and a documentary is concerned with reality.

# Word Analogy Practice

**186.** _____ : plant ::
stable : horse
**a.** cow
**b.** unstable
**c.** oat
**d.** nursery

**187.** dictionary : definition ::
_____ : map
**a.** direction
**b.** south
**c.** atlas
**d.** longitude

**188.** groom : horse ::
_____ : child
**a.** track
**b.** nanny
**c.** gallop
**d.** infantry

**189.** _____ : house ::
anklet : sock
**a.** shoe
**b.** foot
**c.** cottage
**d.** mansion

**190.** annex : _____ ::
insert : book
**a.** shelf
**b.** building
**c.** page
**d.** wing

**191.** _____ : retirement ::
settlement : injury
**a.** golf
**b.** lawyer
**c.** hospital
**d.** pension

**192.** _____ : king ::
bench : judge
  **a.** throne
  **b.** queen
  **c.** court
  **d.** knight

**193.** thumbtack : _____ ::
hook : coat
  **a.** nail
  **b.** poster
  **c.** wall
  **d.** hammer

**194.** hostel : _____ ::
barn : livestock
  **a.** traveler
  **b.** hotel
  **c.** countryside
  **d.** dog

**195.** stratus : cloud ::
_____ : sound
  **a.** murmur
  **b.** lightning
  **c.** thunderous
  **d.** night

**196.** nourish : _____ ::
coddle : comfort
  **a.** feed
  **b.** sleep
  **c.** growth
  **d.** wheat

**197.** _____ : game ::
plagiarize : words
  **a.** crossword
  **b.** poach
  **c.** sports
  **d.** willing

**198.** speech : _____ :: race : track
  **a.** lectern
  **b.** odds
  **c.** preamble
  **d.** tote

**199.** ransom : captive ::
_____ : service
  **a.** prisoner
  **b.** gratuity
  **c.** military
  **d.** restaurant

**200.** glade : _____ ::
castle : moat
  **a.** woods
  **b.** greenish
  **c.** royalty
  **d.** water

**201.** _____ : sheep ::
blight : potato
  **a.** bleat
  **b.** wool
  **c.** rot
  **d.** fold

**202.** _____ : flood ::
helmet : injury
a. drowned
b. Coast Guard
c. river
d. levee

**203.** _____ : team ::
freshman : congress
a. senate
b. player
c. rookie
d. junior

**204.** _____ : bill ::
reimburse : expenses
a. foot
b. doctor
c. charges
d. bond

**205.** _____ : blow :: stain : spill
a. welt
b. wind
c. blotch
d. rug

**206.** laconic : words ::
parched : _____
a. heat
b. moisture
c. desert
d. vapid

**207.** potable : _____ ::
seaworthy : sailing
a. drinking
b. potting
c. portable
d. navigable

**208.** _____ : course ::
menu : meal
a. chef
b. cafeteria
c. colleges
d. syllabus

**209.** _____ : channel ::
flare : accident
a. sinking
b. buoy
c. television
d. river

**210.** indifferent : _____ ::
ardent : zealot
a. stoic
b. altruist
c. cynic
d. zealous

**211.** bulky : streamlined ::
_____ : neat
a. blimp
b. aerodynamic
c. cluttered
d. obese

**212.** slight : hurt :: lag : _____
    **a.** tardiness
    **b.** braggart
    **c.** heft
    **d.** haste

**213.** scruff : neck :: stern : _____
    **a.** lecture
    **b.** dirty
    **c.** boat
    **d.** warning

**214.** valise : _____ :: cask : wine
    **a.** bicycle
    **b.** glass
    **c.** vine
    **d.** clothes

**215.** guileless : cunning ::
shameless : _____
    **a.** modesty
    **b.** guile
    **c.** winning
    **d.** shameful

**216.** fist : hand :: _____ : loop
    **a.** wave
    **b.** rings
    **c.** circuit
    **d.** foot

**217.** brethren : sect ::
actors : _____
    **a.** company
    **b.** church
    **c.** liturgy
    **d.** stagehand

**218.** bonsai : _____ ::
sequoia : forest
    **a.** leaf
    **b.** sunshine
    **c.** hibiscus
    **d.** pot

**219.** pylon : _____ ::
baton : orchestra
    **a.** traffic
    **b.** orange
    **c.** safety
    **d.** clarinet

**220.** logorrhea : words ::
_____ : money
    **a.** cash
    **b.** wealth
    **c.** mint
    **d.** pesos

**221.** chagrin : criticism ::
sag : _____
    **a.** cringe
    **b.** pressure
    **c.** nag
    **d.** redress

**222.** aglet : shoelace ::
nose : _____
    **a.** smell
    **b.** eye
    **c.** face
    **d.** proboscis

**223.** heliotrope : _____ ::
turnover : pastry
a. cake
b. angel
c. candle
d. shrub

**224.** _____ : deciduous ::
pine : coniferous
a. tree
b. oak
c. forest
d. cone

**225.** folderol : _____ ::
benevolence : charity
a. cash
b. greed
c. nonsense
d. event

# Answers

**186.** **d.** A **nursery** houses plants, and a stable houses horses.

**187.** **c.** A dictionary is a book containing definitions, and an **atlas** contains maps.

**188.** **b.** A groom takes care of a horse, and a **nanny** takes care of a child.

**189.** **c.** A **cottage** is a smaller version of a house, and an anklet is a smaller version of sock.

**190.** **b.** An annex is a structure added to a **building**, and an insert is something added to a book.

**191.** **d.** A **pension** is money awarded after retirement, and a settlement is money awarded after an injury.

**192.** **a.** A **throne** is the seat of a king, and a judge sits on the bench.

**193.** **b.** A thumbtack is used to hang a **poster**, and a hook is used to hang a coat.

**194.** **a.** A hostel is used as shelter for **travelers**, and a barn is used as shelter for livestock.

**195.** **a.** Stratus is a type of low cloud formation, and **murmur** is a low sound.

**196.** **c.** To nourish is to encourage **growth**, and to coddle is to encourage comfort.

**197.** **b.** To **poach** means to take someone else's property and call it your own, and to plagiarize is to take someone else's words and call them your own.

**198.** **a.** A speech takes place at a **lectern**, and a race takes place at a track.

**199.** **b.** Ransom is money paid for a captive, and **gratuity** is money paid for a service.

**200.** **a.** A glade is surrounded by **woods**, and a castle is surrounded by a moat.

**201.** **c.** **Rot** is a disease that strikes sheep, and blight is a disease that strikes potatoes.

**202.** **d.** A **levee** prevents a flood, and a helmet prevents injury.

**203.** **c.** A **rookie** is a new member of a sports team; a freshman is a new representative in Congress.

**204.** **a.** To **foot** means to pay a bill, and to reimburse means to pay for expenses.

**205.** **a.** A **welt** is the result of a blow, and a stain is the result of a spill.

**206.** **b.** Laconic is characterized by a lack of words, and parched is characterized by a lack of **moisture**.

**207.** **a.** Something potable is suitable for **drinking**, and something seaworthy is suitable for sailing.

**208.** **d.** A **syllabus** is a description of a course, and a menu is a description of a meal.

**209.** **b.** A **buoy** is used to mark a channel, and a flare is used to mark an accident.

**210.** **a.** Indifferent describes a **stoic**, and ardent describes a zealot.

**211.** **c.** Bulky is an antonym of streamlined, and **cluttered** is an antonym of neat.

**212.** **a.** To slight causes hurt, and to lag causes **tardiness**.

**213.** **c.** Scruff is the back of the neck, and stern is the back of a **boat**.

**214.** **d.** A valise holds **clothing** and a cask holds wine.

**215.** **a.** To be guileless is to lack cunning, and to be shameless is to lack **modesty**.

**216.** **c.** A fist is a closed hand, and a **circuit** is a closed loop.

**217.** **a.** Brethren means members of an order or sect, and actors are members of a **company**.

**218.** **d.** A bonsai tree is grown in a **pot**, and a sequoia grows in a forest.

**219.** **a.** A pylon is used to direct **traffic**, and a baton is used to direct an orchestra.

**220.** **b.** Logorrhea is an excess of words, and **wealth** is an excess of money.

**221.** **b.** Chagrin can be the result of criticism, and sag is the result of **pressure**.

**222.** **c.** An aglet is part of a shoelace, and nose is part of the **face**.

**223.** **d.** A heliotrope is a type of **shrub**, and a turnover is a type of pastry.

**224.** **b.** **Oak** is an example of a deciduous tree, and pine is an example of a coniferous tree.

**225.** **c.** Folderol is a synonym for **nonsense**, and benevolence is a synonym for charity.

# 7

# Word Analogy Practice

**226.** malice : charity ::
_____ : gloom
  **a.** victim
  **b.** lose
  **c.** glee
  **d.** cloud

**227.** total : partial ::
_____ : smile
  **a.** gums
  **b.** frown
  **c.** expression
  **d.** speak

**228.** colossal : enormous ::
constant : _____
  **a.** huge
  **b.** time
  **c.** faithful
  **d.** lapsed

**229.** whole : _____ :: hole : pit
  **a.** pittance
  **b.** whale
  **c.** donut
  **d.** sum

**230.** _____ : courtroom ::
nurse : hospital
  **a.** writ
  **b.** bailiff
  **c.** doctor
  **d.** law

**231.** bray : _____ :: bark : dog
  **a.** braid
  **b.** tree
  **c.** donkey
  **d.** seal

**232.** armor : combat ::
_____ : sewing
a. flag
b. needle
c. dueling
d. thimble

**233.** decoy : duck :: _____ : fish
a. hook
b. lure
c. pond
d. boat

**234.** barrack : base ::
_____ : desert
a. storm
b. tank
c. test
d. adobe

**235.** scythe : grass ::
_____ : beard
a. hair
b. face
c. skin
d. razor

**236.** Clementine : orange ::
monkey : _____
a. jungle
b. baby
c. ape
d. robot

**237.** lemon : _____ ::
chocolate : sweet
a. citrus
b. tart
c. lure
d. sauce

**238.** mean : average ::
kind : _____
a. hurtful
b. meaning
c. variety
d. kindness

**239.** moray : eel :: morel : _____
a. reel
b. slow
c. fungus
d. aquarium

**240.** stiff : supple :: fierce : _____
a. rigid
b. subtle
c. ferocious
d. tame

**241.** hilt : sword ::
needle : _____
a. tease
b. compass
c. dagger
d. kilt

**242.** often : seldom ::
obsolete : _____
a. antiquated
b. current
c. round
d. mixed

**243.** nosegay : flowers ::
_____ : players
a. tickle
b. fruit
c. team
d. ball

**244.** olfactory : _____ ::
optical : eye
a. nose
b. ear
c. heart
d. vision

**245.** risible : _____ ::
unseen : invisible
a. liquid
b. clean
c. funny
d. above

**246.** swaddle : _____ ::
rattle : shake
a. delay
b. paddle
c. snake
d. envelope

**247.** defer : postpone ::
proffer : _____
a. cause
b. tender
c. avoid
d. infer

**248.** rue : _____ ::
rule : dominate
a. avenue
b. domino
c. regret
d. rules

**249.** abandon : reclaim ::
abate : _____
a. abolish
b. debate
c. rise
d. level

**250.** _____ : tire ::
change : switch
a. fix
b. roadside
c. spare
d. weary

**251.** fatuous : sensible ::
_____ : generic
a. fat
b. lofty
c. specific
d. generous

**252.** baleful : beneficent ::
sparse : _____
a. woeful
b. belligerent
c. corrupt
d. dense

**253.** extend : abridge ::
establish : _____
  **a.** uproot
  **b.** bridge
  **c.** fix
  **d.** make

**254.** curb : spur :: revere : _____
  **a.** flout
  **b.** pout
  **c.** tout
  **d.** shout

**255.** mythical : historical ::
general : _____
  **a.** participatory
  **b.** particular
  **c.** colonel
  **d.** orderly

**256.** surfeit : excess ::
excuse : _____
  **a.** forfeit
  **b.** disallow
  **c.** explanation
  **d.** surface

**257.** at loggerheads : _____ ::
dumbstruck : amazement
  **a.** forest
  **b.** awe
  **c.** disagreement
  **d.** agreement

**258.** canonize : unshroud ::
ignore : _____
  **a.** gape
  **b.** jibe
  **c.** bunk
  **d.** slag

**259.** bona fide : deceit ::
languid : _____
  **a.** action
  **b.** weakness
  **c.** truthful
  **d.** bon mot

**260.** cordon : _____ ::
seam : stitches
  **a.** corduroy
  **b.** troops
  **c.** chicken
  **d.** thread

# Answers

**226.** **c.** Malice is an antonym for charity, and **glee** is an antonym for gloom.

**227.** **b.** Total is an antonym for partial, and **frown** is an antonym for smile.

**228.** **c.** Colossal is a synonym for enormous, and constant is a synonym for **faithful**.

**229.** **d.** Whole is another word for **sum**, and hole is another word for pit.

**230.** **b.** A **bailiff** works in a courtroom, and a nurse works in a hospital.

**231.** **c.** Bray is associated with a **donkey's** cry, and bark is associated with a dog's cry.

**232.** **d.** Armor is worn for protection is combat, and a **thimble** is worn for protection in sewing.

**233.** **b.** A decoy is used to attract a duck, and a **lure** is used to attract fish.

**234.** **d.** A barrack is a structure found on a base, and an **adobe** is a structure found in the desert.

**235.** **d.** A scythe is used to cut grass, and a **razor** cuts a beard.

**236.** **c.** An orange is a larger citrus fruit than a clementine; an **ape** is a larger primate than a monkey.

**237.** **b.** A lemon is **tart** in taste; chocolate is sweet in taste.
Note: lemon is also a citrus fruit, but the relationship between chocolate and sweet makes the parallel choice tart, not citrus.

**238.** **c.** Mean is a synonym for average, and kind is a synonym for **variety**.

**239.** **c.** Moray is a type of eel, and morel is a type of **fungus**.

**240.** **d.** Stiff is an antonym for supple, and fierce is an antonym for **tame**.

**241.** **b.** A hilt is part of a sword, and a needle is part of the **compass**.

**242.** **b.** Often is an antonym for seldom, and obsolete is an antonym for **current**.

**243.** **c.** A nosegay is a group of flowers, and a **team** is a group of players.

**244.** **a.** Olfactory relates to the sense of **smell**, or a nose, and optical relates to vision, or an eye.

**245.** **c.** Risible is a synonym for **funny**, and unseen is a synonym for invisible.

**246.** **d.** To swaddle means to **envelop**, and to rattle means to shake.

**247.** **b.** To defer is a synonym of to postpone, and to proffer is a synonym of to **tender**.

**248.** **c.** To rue means to **regret**, and to rule means to dominate.

**249.** **c.** To abandon is an antonym of to reclaim, and to abate is an antonym of to **rise**.

**250.** **d.** To **weary** means to tire, and to change means to switch.

**251.** **c.** Fatuous is an antonym for sensible, and **specific** is an antonym for generic.

**252.** **d.** Baleful is an antonym for beneficent, and sparse is an antonym for **dense**.

**253.** **a.** To extend is an antonym of to abridge, and to establish is an antonym of to **uproot**.

**254.** **a.** To curb is an antonym of to spur, and to revere is an antonym of to **flout**.

**255.** **b.** Mythical is an antonym for historical, and general is an antonym for **particular**.

**256.** **c.** Surfeit is another word for excess, and excuse is another word for **explanation**.

**257.** **c.** At loggerheads means to be in **disagreement**, and dumbstruck means to be in amazement.

**258.** **a.** Canonize is an antonym for unshroud, and ignore is an antonym for **gape**.

**259.** **a.** Bona fide is characterized by a lack of deceit, and languid is characterized by a lack of **action**.

**260.** **b.** A cordon is a line of **troops**; a seam is a line of stitches.

# Word Analogy Practice

261. din : racket :: quiet : _____
   a. harmony
   b. hush
   c. discord
   d. cacophony

262. comical : _____ ::
   broad : narrow
   a. pathetic
   b. new
   c. joke
   d. hysterical

263. halve : divide :: _____ : tear
   a. pare
   b. half
   c. rip
   d. scour

264. scene : locale ::
   scent : _____
   a. trees
   b. noise
   c. fragrance
   d. local

265. _____ : bed ::
   dome : stadium
   a. post
   b. ottoman
   c. sleep
   d. canopy

266. embassy : ambassador ::
   _____ : eagle
   a. mouse
   b. flag
   c. hawk
   d. nest

**267.** _____ : bullet ::
carat : diamond
a. silver
b. cobalt
c. gun
d. caliber

**268.** unusual : novelty ::
_____ : standard
a. odd
b. novel
c. familiar
d. poem

**269.** mural : wall ::
inscription : _____
a. plaque
b. dedication
c. brush
d. floor

**270.** jalopy : car :: _____ : house
a. driveway
b. dump
c. castle
d. luxury

**271.** duvet : _____ :: beret : head
a. ceiling
b. legs
c. bed
d. neck

**272.** _____ : college ::
mechanic : garage
a. book
b. learning
c. professor
d. engine

**273.** cabana : pool ::
chalet : _____
a. billiards
b. Swiss
c. ocean
d. mountain

**274.** mallet : _____ ::
racket : tennis
a. bowling
b. ball
c. croquet
d. net

**275.** ledger : accounts ::
_____ : observations
a. pundit
b. weather
c. astrology
d. diary

**276.** powerless : efficacious ::
_____ : asocial
a. corrupt
b. hidden
c. social
d. limited

**277.** plume : feather ::
flume : _____
a. duck
b. gorge
c. nest
d. laughter

**278.** _____ : blood ::
viaduct : water
a. stream
b. swim
c. artery
d. plasma

**279.** outlaw : _____ ::
offend : affront
a. chase
b. police
c. crime
d. forbid

**280.** attic : _____ :: crown : head
a. king
b. family
c. stairs
d. house

**281.** enfeeble : fortify ::
concede : _____
a. dispute
b. close
c. expect
d. surrender

**282.** slack : _____ ::
plucky : courageous
a. tight
b. silent
c. negligent
d. cowardly

**283.** impious : _____ ::
indignant : irked
a. furious
b. irreverent
c. irksome
d. unfriendly

**284.** rapier : _____ ::
despot : ruler
a. respite
b. sword
c. paper
d. king

**285.** endure : continue ::
entreat : _____
a. plea
b. segue
c. purchase
d. surrender

**286.** forgo : _____ ::
undo : reverse
a. go
b. begin
c. renounce
d. forget

**287.** jest : earnest ::
esteem : _____
a. just
b. honor
c. disgrace
d. mettle

**288.** perennial : _____ ::
annual : yearly
a. continuous
b. occasional
c. tulip
d. garden

**289.** _____ : ignominy ::
equity : fairness
a. fame
b. shame
c. inequality
d. balance

**290.** confederate : _____ ::
narrator : chronicler
a. north
b. partner
c. history
d. teacher

**291.** _____ : obfuscate ::
hinder : help
a. obscure
b. whip
c. lie
d. explain

**292.** vestige : _____ ::
vestment : garb
a. artery
b. sacrament
c. clergy
d. footprint

**293.** supplicate : _____ ::
replicate : copy
a. borrow
b. beg
c. steal
d. pinch

**294.** invective : abuse ::
imposture : _____
a. sham
b. imposition
c. injection
d. insurrection

**295.** wattle : _____ ::
crust : bread
a. waffle
b. griddle
c. gait
d. neck

# Answers

**261. b.** Din and racket are synonyms, as are quiet and **hush**.

**262. a.** Comical is an antonym for **pathetic**, and broad is an antonym for narrow.

**263. c.** To halve means to divide, and to **rip** means to tear.

**264. c.** Scene is another word for locale, and scent is another word for **fragrance**.

**265. d.** A **canopy** covers a bed, and a dome covers a stadium.

**266. d.** An embassy is the residence of an ambassador, and an eagle lives in a **nest**.

**267. d. Caliber** is a measurement of a bullet, and carat is a measurement of a diamond.

**268. c.** Unusual describes a novelty, and **familiar** describes a standard.

**269. a.** A mural is a painting that appears on a wall, and an inscription appears on a **plaque**.

**270. b.** A jalopy is an old, dilapidated car, and a **dump** is a term for a dilapidated house.

**271. c.** A duvet goes on a **bed**, and a beret goes on a head.

**272. c.** A **professor** works at a college, and a mechanic works at a garage.

**273. d.** A cabana can be found near a pool, and a chalet is found near a **mountain**.

**274. c.** A mallet is used to play **croquet**, and a racket is used to play tennis.

**275.** **d.** A ledger is a book that contains accounts, and a **diary** is a book that contains observations.

**276.** **c.** Powerless is an antonym for efficacious, and **social** is an antonym for asocial.

**277.** **b.** A plume is a feather, and a flume is a **gorge**.

**278.** **c.** An **artery** carries blood, and a viaduct carries water.

**279.** **d.** To outlaw is another word for to **forbid**, and to offend is another word for to affront.

**280.** **d.** An attic is the upper part of a **house**, and the crown is the upper part of the head.

**281.** **a.** To enfeeble is an antonym of to fortify, and to concede is an antonym of to **dispute**.

**282.** **c.** Slack is a synonym for **negligent**, and plucky is a synonym for courageous.

**283.** **b.** Impious means **irreverent**, and indignant means irked.

**284.** **b.** A rapier is a type of **sword**, and a despot is a type of ruler.

**285.** **a.** To endure means to continue, and to entreat means to **plead**.

**286.** **c.** To forgo is another word for to **renounce**, and to undo is another word for to reverse.

**287.** **c.** Jest is an antonym for earnest, and esteem is an antonym for **disgrace**.

**288.** **a.** A perennial is a **continuous** occurrence, and an annual is a yearly occurrence.

**289.** **b.** **Shame** is a synonym for ignominy, and equity is a synonym for fairness.

**290.** **b.** A confederate is a synonym for a **partner**, and a narrator is a synonym for a chronicler.

**291.** **d.** To **explain** is an antonym of to obfuscate, and to hinder is an antonym of to help.

**292.** **d.** Vestige is another word for **footprint**, and vestment is another word for garb.

**293.** **b.** To supplicate is a synonym of to **beg**, and to replicate is a synonym of to copy.

**294.** **a.** Invective is a synonym for abuse, and imposture is a synonym for **sham**.

**295.** **d.** The wattle is part of the **neck**, and crust is part of bread.

# Word Analogy Practice

**296.** drum : instrument ::
drill : _____
   **a.** hammer
   **b.** oven
   **c.** tool
   **d.** crescendo

**297.** peak : mountain ::
_____ : house
   **a.** maximize
   **b.** roof
   **c.** porch
   **d.** bungalow

**298.** sheet : pad :: flower : _____
   **a.** card
   **b.** gift
   **c.** petal
   **d.** bouquet

**299.** arid : desert :: _____ : space
   **a.** night
   **b.** western
   **c.** vast
   **d.** star

**300.** glasses : _____ ::
bicycle : unicycle
   **a.** helmet
   **b.** pedal
   **c.** speeds
   **d.** monocle

**301.** _____ : real ::
hostile : friendly
   **a.** very
   **b.** lure
   **c.** true
   **d.** imaginary

**302.** precinct : city ::
chapter : _____
  **a.** policeman
  **b.** sentence
  **c.** charge
  **d.** book

**303.** pilgrim : journey ::
recluse : _____
  **a.** ocean
  **b.** home
  **c.** space
  **d.** Thanksgiving

**304.** vestibule : building ::
_____ : house
  **a.** foyer
  **b.** verranda
  **c.** porch
  **d.** yard

**305.** seal : wax :: _____ : cork
  **a.** stopper
  **b.** bottle
  **c.** dolphin
  **d.** envelope

**306.** reconcile : fight ::
_____ : procrastinate
  **a.** hurry
  **b.** stall
  **c.** cover
  **d.** shun

**307.** _____ : cocoa ::
omelet : egg
  **a.** toast
  **b.** coffee
  **c.** brownies
  **d.** pizza

**308.** _____ : sign :: sink : dip
  **a.** drop
  **b.** slip
  **c.** ink
  **d.** drink

**309.** AC : alternating current ::
DC : _____
  **a.** diverse current
  **b.** direct current
  **c.** diode charge
  **d.** dived cell

**310.** _____ : spiel :: snarl : mess
  **a.** spill
  **b.** pitch
  **c.** spool
  **d.** sputter

**311.** epaulet : shoulder ::
cravat : _____
  **a.** head
  **b.** arm
  **c.** neck
  **d.** foot

**312.** rancor : enmity ::
languor : _____
  **a.** rank
  **b.** language
  **c.** sympathy
  **d.** lethargy

**313.** fibula : leg :: _____ : arm
- **a.** ulna
- **b.** sternum
- **c.** pelvis
- **d.** tibia

**314.** babble : language ::
static : _____
- **a.** sock
- **b.** truce
- **c.** word
- **d.** transmission

**315.** _____ : epigram ::
sweeping : epic
- **a.** concise
- **b.** massive
- **c.** elliptical
- **d.** wordy

**316.** brew : _____ :: fret : worry
- **a.** drink
- **b.** bar
- **c.** wipe
- **d.** contrive

**317.** _____ : tailored ::
gallant : brave
- **a.** logical
- **b.** fortuitous
- **c.** sartorial
- **d.** homemade

**318.** _____ : soup :: latex : paint
- **a.** spoon
- **b.** spill
- **c.** heat
- **d.** stock

**319.** queue : _____ ::
query : question
- **a.** quiz
- **b.** spy
- **c.** line
- **d.** surprise

**320.** succor : _____ :: ire : anger
- **a.** aid
- **b.** offense
- **c.** flavor
- **d.** sleep

**321.** mythologize : debunk ::
exile : _____
- **a.** stranger
- **b.** welcome
- **c.** push
- **d.** exit

**322.** abate : reduce ::
beat : _____
- **a.** surpass
- **b.** rebate
- **c.** deduce
- **d.** encompass

**323.** _____ : ash :: shard : glass
- **a.** furnace
- **b.** smoke
- **c.** water
- **d.** cinder

**324.** mynah : bird ::
terrapin : _____
- **a.** hemisphere
- **b.** beak
- **c.** snake
- **d.** turtle

**325.** bathysphere : _____ ::
telescope : astronomer
a. sea
b. tub
c. oceanographer
d. universe

**326.** spelunker : _____ ::
astronomer : space
a. spaceship
b. light
c. cave
d. wave

**327.** adore : abhor ::
censure : _____
a. complain
b. count
c. extol
d. question

**328.** channel : waterway ::
_____ : fabric
a. polyester
b. zipper
c. cotton
d. stone

**329.** _____ : carousel ::
bullet : cylinder
a. carnival
b. rifle
c. slide
d. cone

**330.** _____ : urge ::
enthrall : interest
a. confuse
b. disagree
c. exhort
d. enjoy

# Answers

**296.** **c.** A drum is a type of instrument, and drill is a type of **tool**.

**297.** **b.** The peak is the top of a mountain, and the **roof** is the top of a house.

**298.** **d.** A sheet is a part of a pad of paper, and a flower is part of a **bouquet**.

**299.** **c.** Arid describes a desert, and **vast** describes space.

**300.** **d.** A **monocle** has one lens while glasses have two lenses, and a unicycle has one wheel while a bicycle has two wheels.

**301.** **d.** **Imaginary** is the opposite of real, and hostile is the opposite of friendly.

**302.** **d.** A precinct is a division of a city, and a chapter is a division of a **book**.

**303.** **b.** A pilgrim can be found on a journey, and a recluse can be found at **home**.

**304.** **a.** A vestibule is the entrance to a building, and a **foyer** is the entrance to a home.

**305.** **a.** A seal is made of wax, and a **stopper** is made of cork.

**306.** **a.** Reconcile is an antonym of fight, and **hurry** is an antonym of procrastinate.

**307.** **c.** **Brownies** have cocoa as an ingredient, and an omelet has eggs as an ingredient.

**308.** **c.** To **ink** means to sign, and to sink means to dip.

**309.** **b.** AC stands for alternating current, and DC stands for **direct current**.

**310.** b. **Pitch** is a synonym for spiel, and snarl is a synonym for mess.

**311.** c. An epaulet is worn on the shoulder, and a cravat is worn on the **neck**.

**312.** d. Rancor is a synonym for enmity, and languor is a synonym for **lethargy**.

**313.** a. The fibula is a bone in the leg, and the **ulna** is a bone in the arm.

**314.** d. Babble is garbled language, and static is a garbled **transmission**.

**315.** a. **Concise** describes an epigram, and sweeping describes an epic.

**316.** d. To brew means to **contrive**, and to fret means to worry.

**317.** c. **Sartorial** is a synonym for tailored, and gallant is a synonym for brave.

**318.** d. **Stock** is the base of soup, and latex is the base of paint.

**319.** c. A queue is another word for a **line**, and a query is another word for a question.

**320.** a. Succor means help or **aid**, and ire means anger.

**321.** b. Mythologize is an antonym of debunk, and exile is an antonym of **welcome**.

**322.** a. Abate and reduce are synonyms, as are beat and **surpass**.

**323.** d. A **cinder** is a fragment of ash, and a shard is a fragment of glass..

**324.** d. A **mynah** is a type of bird, and a terrapin is a type of turtle.

**325.** c. A bathyshere is used by an **oceanographer**, and a telescope is used by an astronomer.

**326.** **c.** A spelunker is someone explores **caves**, and an astronomer is someone who explores space.

**327.** **c.** To adore is the opposite of abhor, and to censure is the opposite of **extol**.

**328.** **c.** A channel is a natural waterway, and **cotton** is a natural fabric.

**329.** **c.** A **slide** (photographic transparency) goes into a carousel, and a bullet goes into a cylinder.

**330.** **c.** To **exhort** is to urge strongly, and to enthrall is to interest strongly.

# 10

# Word Analogy Practice

**331.** quick : slow ::
youthful : _____
  **a.** immature
  **b.** aged
  **c.** child
  **d.** adult

**332.** deference : elder ::
indifference : _____
  **a.** defendant
  **b.** child
  **c.** stranger
  **d.** judge

**333.** parsley : garnish ::
salt : _____
  **a.** pepper
  **b.** seasoning
  **c.** grain
  **d.** parsnip

**334.** pitch : throw :: heat : _____
  **a.** sun
  **b.** strike
  **c.** warm
  **d.** hit

**335.** shaft : spear :: neck : _____
  **a.** sleeve
  **b.** guitar
  **c.** sound
  **d.** blood

**336.** _____ : future ::
historian : past
  **a.** date
  **b.** seer
  **c.** book
  **d.** general

**337.** shadow : trail ::
_____ : disgrace
a. litter
b. forest
c. hike
d. shame

**338.** protractor : angle ::
ruler : _____
a. rectangle
b. length
c. classroom
d. king

**339.** _____ : nine ::
pentagon : five
a. nonagon
b. hexagon
c. septum
d. octagon

**340.** rack : _____ :: tack : sailing
a. billiards
b. scubadiving
c. railing
d. boating

**341.** phenomenon : phenomena ::
die : _____
a. heaven
b. miracle
c. dice
d. phenomenal

**342.** brag : garb :: drab : _____
a. mundane
b. actor
c. costume
d. bard

**343.** prim : _____ ::
grim : somber
a. timid
b. probable
c. neat
d. primary

**344.** _____ : water :: tree : sap
a. fire
b. forest
c. nourishment
d. hydrant

**345.** tricycle : wheel ::
_____ : month
a. August
b. day
c. perennial
d. trimester

**346.** limp : injury ::
_____ : conviction
a. stumble
b. inflammation
c. rest
d. incarceration

**347.** _____ : arm ::
column : ceiling
a. leg
b. sling
c. floor
d. wing

**348.** partisan : biased ::
_____ : limited
  **a.** first
  **b.** balanced
  **c.** dogged
  **d.** finite

**349.** deduce : infer ::
_____ : crow
  **a.** boast
  **b.** infuriate
  **c.** soar
  **d.** reduce

**350.** resin : _____ ::
gelatin : preserves
  **a.** raisin
  **b.** cream
  **c.** varnish
  **d.** pudding

**351.** hydric : moist ::
_____ : burning
  **a.** tonic
  **b.** sciatic
  **c.** phlegmatic
  **d.** pyric

**352.** thresher : _____ ::
mastiff : dog
  **a.** robin
  **b.** master
  **c.** shark
  **d.** policeman

**353.** garble : distort ::
garner : _____
  **a.** learn
  **b.** warble
  **c.** earn
  **d.** distress

**354.** yeomanly : _____ ::
perilous : safe
  **a.** awkward
  **b.** disloyal
  **c.** true
  **d.** seaworthy

**355.** parrot : mimic ::
dog : _____
  **a.** canine
  **b.** talk
  **c.** cat
  **d.** hound

**356.** breach : _____ :: fly : bird
  **a.** seagull
  **b.** beach
  **c.** whale
  **d.** foam

**357.** infuse : permeate ::
kindle : _____
  **a.** light
  **b.** grow
  **c.** steep
  **d.** pound

**358.** reprove : _____ ::
approve : sanction
a. policy
b. chide
c. testify
d. cancel

**359.** defy : obey ::
_____ : placate
a. please
b. aggravate
c. submit
d. change

**360.** baste : cooking ::
_____ : gardening
a. pinch
b. mulch
c. heat
d. paste

**361.** persist : _____ ::
eject : welcome
a. habituate
b. quit
c. torment
d. pest

**362.** fuzzy : clarity ::
_____ : flexibility
a. flexible
b. rigid
c. clear
d. forthright

**363.** _____ : heavy ::
ravenous : hungry
a. light
b. leaden
c. slow
d. boss

**364.** festoon : chain ::
creek : _____
a. stream
b. inlay
c. crook
d. island

**365.** theology : religion ::
phenology : _____
a. pheremones
b. psychology
c. climate
d. geology

**366.** Machiavellian : _____ ::
Orwellian : intrusive
a. unscrupulous
b. disconsolate
c. sincere
d. penurious

**367.** physics : _____ ::
eugenics : heredity
a. earthquakes
b. matter
c. poetry
d. sonatas

**368.** _____ : static ::
deficient : complete
  **a.** clinging
  **b.** electric
  **c.** alive
  **d.** kinetic

**369.** sagacious : undiscerning ::
amusing : _____
  **a.** clever
  **b.** droll
  **c.** humorless
  **d.** confusing

**370.** inchoate : _____ ::
gainful : worthwhile
  **a.** incoherent
  **b.** profitable
  **c.** unfinished
  **d.** choosy

# Answers

**331.** **b.** Quick is the opposite of slow, and youthful is the opposite of **aged**.

**332.** **c.** Deference is shown to an elder, and indifference is shown to a **stranger**.

**333.** **b.** Parsley is used as a garnish, and salt is used as a **seasoning**.

**334.** **c.** To pitch is a synonym of to throw, and to heat is a synonym of to **warm**.

**335.** **b.** The shaft is part of a spear, and the neck is part of the **guitar**.

**336.** **b.** A **seer** looks into the future, and a historian looks into the past.

**337.** **d.** To shadow is to trail someone, and to **shame** is to disgrace someone.

**338.** **b.** A protractor is used to measure an angle, and a ruler is used to measure **length**.

**339.** **a.** A **nonagon** is a polygon with nine sides, and a pentagon is a polygon with five sides.

**340.** **a.** **Rack** is a term used in billiards, and tack is a term used in sailing.

**341.** **c.** Phenomenon is the singular of phenomena, and die is the singular of **dice**.

**342.** **d.** Brag is the palindrome of garb, and drab is the palindrome of **bard**.

**343.** **c.** Prim is a synonym for **neat**, and grim is a synonym for somber.

**344.** **d.** A **hydrant** is a source of water, and a tree is a source of sap.

**345.** **d.** A tricycle has three wheels, and a **trimester** is three months.

**346.** **d.** A limp is the result of an injury, and **incarceration** is the result of a conviction.

**347.** **b.** A sling is used to support an **arm**, and a column is used to support a ceiling.

**348.** **d.** Partisan is a synonym for biased, and **finite** is a synonym for limited.

**349.** **a.** Deduce is a synonym of infer, and **boast** is a synonym of crow.

**350.** **c.** Resin is used in making **varnishes**, and gelatin is used in making preserves.

**351.** **d.** Hydric is associated with something moist, and **pyric** is associated with something burning.

**352.** **c.** Thresher is a type of **shark**, and mastiff is a type of dog.

**353.** **c.** Garble means distort, and garner means **earn**.

**354.** **b.** Yeomanly is an antonym for **disloyal**, and perilous is an antonym for safe.

**355.** **d.** To parrot means to mimic, and to dog means to **hound**.

**356.** **c.** Breaching is a movement made by **whales**, and flying is a movement made by birds.

**357.** **a.** Infuse means permeate, and kindle means **light**.

**358.** **b.** Reprove is a synonym of **chide**, and approve is a synonym of sanction.

**359.** **b.** To defy is the opposite of to obey, and to **aggravate** is the opposite of to placate.

**360.** **b.** Baste is a cooking term, and **mulch** is a gardening term.

**361.** **b.** To persist is the opposite of to **quit**, and to eject is the opposite of to welcome.

**362.** **b.** Fuzzy means lacking in clarity, and **rigid** means lacking flexibility.

**363.** **b.** To be **leaden** is to be oppressively heavy, and to be ravenous is to be excessively hungry.

**364.** **a.** A festoon is another word for a decorative chain, and a creek is another word for an **stream**.

**365.** **c.** Theology is the study of religion, and phenology is the study of **climate**.

**366.** **a.** Something Machiavellian is considered **unscrupulous**, and Orwellian describes something as intrusive.

**367.** **b.** Physics is a science that deals with **matter**, and eugenics is a science that deals with heredity.

**368.** **d.** **Kinetic** means to be in motion and static means to be at rest, and deficient means lacking and complete means to be whole.

**369.** **c.** To be sagacious is to be the opposite of undiscerning and to be amusing is to be the opposite of **humorless**.

**370.** **c.** Inchoate is a synonym for **unfinished**, and gainful is a synonym for worthwhile.

# 11

# Word Analogy Practice

**371.** luge : _____ :: toe : tone
 **a.** ski
 **b.** lane
 **c.** lunge
 **d.** feet

**372.** pool : loop :: lap : _____
 **a.** lifeguard
 **b.** track
 **c.** heat
 **d.** pal

**373.** _____ : enunciate ::
 praise : insult
 **a.** upbraid
 **b.** umbrage
 **c.** mumble
 **d.** broadcast

**374.** turban : _____ ::
 turbine : engine
 **a.** robe
 **b.** toga
 **c.** headdress
 **d.** nomad

**375.** trellis : garden ::
 fireplace : _____
 **a.** smoke
 **b.** house
 **c.** log
 **d.** ash

**376.** slither : snake ::
 rotate : _____
 **a.** rock
 **b.** support
 **c.** fan
 **d.** turn

**377.** eraser : pencil :: _____ : pen
a. write
b. delete
c. nib
d. calligraphy

**378.** _____ : 1.5 :: $\frac{1}{2}$ : 0.5
a. 5
b. $\frac{2}{1}$
c. 1
d. $\frac{3}{2}$

**379.** _____ : armor ::
equipment : gear
a. horse
b. divine
c. mask
d. shield

**380.** purr : _____ ::
huff : indignation
a. cat
b. whiff
c. contentment
d. anger

**381.** lap : pool :: _____ : space
a. pass
b. gene
c. light-year
d. slide

**382.** lithe : _____ ::
slovenly : slob
a. filth
b. asleep
c. giant
d. dancer

**383.** game : series ::
_____ : word
a. winner
b. sentence
c. syllable
d. event

**384.** _____ : cut ::
flowers : bloom
a. snip
b. bouquet
c. teeth
d. excise

**385.** _____ : land :: slice : cake
a. earth
b. fly
c. mud
d. acre

**386.** 6 : 5 :: 30 : _____
a. 36
b. 29
c. 35
d. 9

**387.** brig : _____ :: sham : hoax
a. limerick
b. crate
c. prison
d. trickery

**388.** dolly : _____ ::
ferry : passenger
a. ticket
b. ship
c. camera
d. ocean

**389.** prosaic : _____ ::
profuse : lush
a. ordinary
b. tropical
c. abundant
d. sparse

**390.** _____ : zero ::
ampersand : and
a. goat
b. zephyr
c. cipher
d. champion

**391.** scratch : race ::
_____ : poker
a. draw
b. king
c. card
d. fold

**392.** _____ : hidden ::
ebullient : glum
a. sudden
b. gloomy
c. overt
d. off

**393.** gloaming : _____ ::
bearing : manner
a. gloom
b. beaming
c. morning
d. dusk

**394.** irreverent : respect ::
slipshod : _____
a. messy
b. slippery
c. care
d. wit

**395.** _____ : leave ::
vacillate : decide
a. linger
b. arrive
c. announce
d. depart

**396.** receipt : _____ ::
license : marriage
a. money
b. store
c. purchase
d. husband

**397.** efficient : wasteful ::
_____ : deceptive
a. sly
b. detective
c. honest
d. cautious

**398.** finesse : cunning ::
_____ : resentment
a. agility
b. vision
c. purpose
d. jealousy

**399.** battalion : _____ ::
dollar : cent
a. army
b. troop
c. rifles
d. battle

**400.** pilot : _____ ::
doctor : repair
a. airplane
b. guide
c. driver
d. license

**401.** cineast : film ::
gastronome : _____
a. gnomes
b. files
c. food
d. stars

**402.** _____ : spoil :: walk : path
a. hike
b. grass
c. mold
d. trail

**403.** osier : _____ ::
paper : origami
a. artisan
b. basketry
c. ancient
d. needlepoint

**404.** scimitar : _____ ::
revolver : gun
a. saber
b. bullet
c. vest
d. soldier

**405.** Rivera : murals ::
_____ : mobiles
a. Degas
b. Hopper
c. Matisse
d. Calder

**406.** mandible : jaw ::
metatarsal : _____
a. chew
b. chest
c. foot
d. neck

**407.** _____ : bow :: stumble : fall
a. truckle
b. trickle
c. tickle
d. tuck

**408.** manacle : hands ::
_____ : feet
a. shin
b. fetter
c. stock
d. fodder

**409.** _____ : fez ::
pom-pom : tam-o'-shanter
  **a.** red
  **b.** Morocco
  **c.** guard
  **d.** tassel

**410.** flip : impertinent ::
dice : _____
  **a.** cut
  **b.** cards
  **c.** bounce
  **d.** gamble

# Answers

**371.** c. Luge with an added "n" is **lunge**, and toe with an added "n" is tone.

**372.** d. Pool is loop spelled backward, and lap is **pal** in reverse.

**373.** c. To **mumble** is the opposite of to enunciate, and to praise is the opposite of to insult.

**374.** c. A turban is a type of **headdress**, and a turbine is a type of engine.

**375.** b. A trellis is found in a garden, and a fireplace is found in a **house**.

**376.** c. Slither describes the movement of a snake, and rotate describes the movement of a **fan**.

**377.** c. The eraser is part of a pencil, and the **nib** is part of a pen.

**378.** d. $\frac{3}{2}$ is the same as 1.5, and $\frac{1}{2}$ is the same as 0.5.

**379.** d. A **shield** is a synonym of armor, and equipment is a synonym of gear.

**380.** c. To purr is a sign of **contentment**, and to huff is a sign of indignation.

**381.** c. Lap is a distance covered in a pool, and **light-year** is a distance covered in space.

**382.** d. Lithe can describe a **dancer**, and slovenly can describe a slob.

**383.** c. A game is part of a series, and a **syllable** is part of a word.

**384.** c. **Teeth** cut and flowers bloom.

**385.** d. An **acre** is a piece of land, and a slice is a piece of cake.

**386.** **b.** 6 minus 1 is 5, and 30 minus 1 is **29**.

**387.** **c.** A brig is another word for a **prison**, and a sham is another word for a hoax.

**388.** **c.** A dolly moves a television or motion picture **camera**, and a ferry moves passengers.

**389.** **a.** Prosaic means **ordinary**, and profuse means lush.

**390.** **c.** A **cipher** is a symbol for a zero, and an ampersand is a symbol for *and*.

**391.** **d.** To scratch is to withdraw from a race, and to **fold** is to withdraw from poker.

**392.** **c.** **Overt** is an antonym of hidden, and ebullient is an antonym of glum.

**393.** **d.** Gloaming is another word for **dusk**, and bearing is another word for manner.

**394.** **c.** Irreverent means lacking in respect, and slipshod means lacking in **care**.

**395.** **a.** To **linger** means to be slow to leave, and to vacillate is to be slow to decide.

**396.** **c.** A receipt is an acknowledgement or document of a **purchase**, and a license is a document acknowledging a marriage.

**397.** **c.** To be efficient is the opposite of wasteful, and to be **honest** is the opposite of deceptive.

**398.** **d.** Finesse is a synonym for cunning, and **jealousy** is a synonym for resentment.

**399.** **b.** A **troop** is a unit of a battalion, and a cent is a unit of a dollar.

**400.** b. To pilot means to **guide**, and to doctor means to repair.

**401.** c. A cineast loves film, and a gastronome loves **food**.

**402.** c. **Mold** is a synonym for spoil, and walk is a synonym for path.

**403.** b. Osier is a willow used to make **baskets**, and paper is used to make origami.

**404.** a. A scimitar is a **saber**, and a revolver is a gun.

**405.** d. Diego Rivera was an artist known for his murals, and Alexander **Calder** was known for his mobiles.

**406.** c. The mandible is part of the jaw, and the metatarsal is part of the **foot**.

**407.** a. To **truckle** means to bow, and to stumble means to fall.

**408.** b. A manacle is a shackle for the hands, and a **fetter** is a shackle for the feet.

**409.** d. A **tassel** is part of a fez, and a pom-pom is part of a tam-o'-shanter.

**410.** a. Flip is a synonym for impertinent, and dice is a synonym of **cut**.

# 12

# Challenging Word Analogy Practice

**411.** cheap : peach ::
_____ : large
a. king
b. regal
c. orange
d. majestic

**412.** 4 : _____ :: 3 : 9
a. 6
b. 27
c. 16
d. 64

**413.** worth : whort ::
_____ : nadir
a. apex
b. arc
c. drain
d. sink

**414.** development : sprawl ::
famine : _____
a. malnutrition
b. crawl
c. urban
d. obesity

**415.** to : too :: loot : _____
a. two
b. steal
c. toot
d. lute

**416.** member : club ::
_____ : pride
a. lion
b. win
c. medal
d. accept

**417.** haste : waste ::
_____ : crowd
a. fast
b. three
c. group
d. makes

**418.** whoop : exuberance ::
keen : _____
a. whoops
b. neat
c. mourning
d. diffidence

**419.** purse : super :: plea : _____
a. avoid
b. charity
c. help
d. leap

**420.** _____ : rainfall ::
condensation : humidity
a. erosion
b. cloud
c. ground
d. forecast

**421.** reveille : _____ ::
taps : lights out
a. dance
b. sunrise
c. night
d. awaken

**422.** cruiseliner : passengers ::
_____ : books
a. agent
b. author
c. volume
d. library

**423.** no : know :: steal : _____
a. rob
b. negative
c. steel
d. don't

**424.** _____ : navigation ::
abacus : calculation
a. circumference
b. automation
c. sextant
d. hydration

**425.** 6 : _____ :: 8 : 18
a. 2
b. 10
c. 12
d. 16

**426.** binge : begin :: tea : _____
a. supper
b. coffee
c. eat
d. water

**427.** son : sun :: _____ : sew
a. so
b. sob
c. needle
d. daughter

**428.** _____ : draw :: list : silt
   **a.** drawing
   **b.** ward
   **c.** sludge
   **d.** lean

**429.** cabal : _____ ::
   output : yield
   **a.** plot
   **b.** plant
   **c.** cable
   **d.** stop

**430.** dither : settle ::
   display : _____
   **a.** corrupt
   **b.** bother
   **c.** hide
   **d.** count

**431.** _____ : patois ::
   plot : design
   **a.** tiding
   **b.** mystery
   **c.** patio
   **d.** jargon

**432.** _____ : entertain ::
   bully : browbeat
   **a.** miser
   **b.** raconteur
   **c.** harmonious
   **d.** felon

**433.** _____ : trumpet ::
   fret : guitar
   **a.** song
   **b.** valve
   **c.** trombone
   **d.** band

**434.** hamstring : _____ ::
   stake : bet
   **a.** ride
   **b.** cripple
   **c.** scratch
   **d.** wager

**435.** _____ : frame ::
   mosaic : tile
   **a.** film
   **b.** engraving
   **c.** bathroom
   **d.** decoration

**436.** badger : annoy ::
   _____ : dispute
   **a.** fox
   **b.** quarrel
   **c.** point
   **d.** reconcile

**437.** exasperate : irk ::
   _____ : dissuade
   **a.** prevent
   **b.** leather
   **c.** argue
   **d.** dismiss

**438.** histrionic : _____ ::
didactic : teacher
a. history
b. mechanic
c. actor
d. debate

**439.** lock : canal :: dock : _____
a. courtroom
b. locksmith
c. ear
d. duck

**440.** wildcat : _____ ::
forage : food
a. bobcat
b. game
c. mountain
d. oil

**441.** clumsy : dexterity ::
_____ : will
a. passive
b. oaf
c. submit
d. wish

**442.** drudgery : work ::
cacophony : _____
a. noise
b. orchestra
c. telephone
d. dissonance

**443.** _____ : wheat ::
lentil : legume
a. thyme
b. rice
c. tofu
d. spelt

**444.** hector : _____ ::
foil : thwart
a. bait
b. shun
c. embrace
d. trail

**445.** bow : obeisance ::
objective : _____
a. salute
b. worship
c. goal
d. subjective

**446.** probity : _____ ::
probability : likelihood
a. honesty
b. prohibition
c. inquisition
d. eventuality

**447.** mnemonics : _____ ::
phonetics : language
a. memory
b. future
c. hieroglyphics
d. movement

**448.** cask : sack :: thin : _____
   **a.** fire
   **b.** satchel
   **c.** rope
   **d.** hint

**449.** perfidy : _____ ::
satire : parody
   **a.** treachery
   **b.** humor
   **c.** forgiveness
   **d.** performance

**450.** _____ : plangent ::
contemptible : estimable
   **a.** pungent
   **b.** quiet
   **c.** noisy
   **d.** combustible

# Answers

**411.** **b.** Cheap is an anagram for peach, and **regal** is an anagram for large.

**412.** **c.** 4 squared is **16**, and 3 squared is 9.

**413.** **c.** Worth is an anagram for whort, and **drain** is an anagram for nadir.

**414.** **a.** Development is a cause of sprawl, and famine is a cause of **malnutrition**.

**415.** **d.** Too is a homophone for to, and loot is a homophone for **lute**.

**416.** **a.** A member is part of a club, and a **lion** is part of a pride.

**417.** **b.** According to well-known proverbs, haste makes waste, and **three** is a crowd.

**418.** **c.** A whoop is a sound of exuberance; a keen is a sound of **mourning**.

**419.** **d.** Purse is an anagram for super, and plea is an anagram for **leap**.

**420.** **a.** **Erosion** is a result of rainfall, and condensation is a result of humidity.

**421.** **d.** Reveille is a musical signal to **awaken**, and taps is a musical signal for lights out.

**422.** **d.** A cruiseliner houses passengers, and a **library** houses books.

**423.** **c.** No is a homophone for know, and steal is a homophone for **steel**.

**424.** **c.** A **sextant** is a tool used in navigation, and an abacus is a tool used in calculation.

**425.** **d.** 6 plus 10 is **16**, and 8 plus 10 is 18.

**426.** **c.** Binge is an anagram for begin, and tea is an anagram for **eat**.

**427.** **a.** Son is a homophone for sun, and **so** is a homophone for sew.

**428.** **b.** **Ward** is an anagram for draw, and list is an anagram for silt.

**429.** **a.** Cabal is a synonym for **plot**, and output is a synonym for yield.

**430.** **c.** Dither is an antonym for settle, and display is an antonym for **hide**.

**431.** **d.** **Jargon** is a synonym for patois, and plot is a synonym for design.

**432.** **b.** A **raconteur** is someone who entertains, and a bully is someone who browbeats.

**433.** **b.** A **valve** is part of a trumpet, and a fret is part of a guitar.

**434.** **b.** To hamstring means to **cripple**, and to stake means to bet.

**435.** **a.** A **film** is composed of individual frames, and a mosaic is composed of individual tiles.

**436.** **b.** To badger is to annoy persistently, and to **quarrel** is to dispute actively.

**437.** **a.** To exasperate is to irk entirely, and to **prevent** is to dissuade entirely.

**438.** **c.** Histrionic describes the behavior of an **actor**, and didactic describes a teacher.

**439.** **a.** A lock is found in a canal, and a dock is found in a **courtroom**.

**440.** **d.** To wildcat means to look for **oil**, and to forage means to look for food.

**441.** **a.** Clumsy means lacking dexterity, and **passive** means lacking in will.

**442.** **a.** Drudgery is unpleasant work, and cacophony is unpleasant **noise**.

**443.** **d.** **Spelt** is a wheat, and a lentil is a legume.

**444.** **a.** Hector is a synonym of **bait**, and foil is a synonym for thwart.

**445.** **c.** A bow is a synonym for an obeisance, and an objective is a synonym for a **goal**.

**446.** **a.** Probity means **honesty**, and probability means likelihood.

**447.** **a.** Mnemonics deals with **memory**, and phonetics deals with language.

**448.** **d.** Cask is an anagram for sack, and thin is an anagram for **hint**.

**449.** **a.** Perfidy is a synonym for **treachery**, and satire is a synonym for parody.

**450.** **b.** **Quiet** is an antonym for plangent, and contemptible is an antonym for estimable.

# 13

## Targeted Word Analogy Practice for the Miller Analogies Test (MAT)

**451.** 1/3 : 2/3 :: _____ : 60
    **a.** 20
    **b.** 30
    **c.** 10
    **d.** 120

**452.** sari : India ::
    _____ : Mexico
    **a.** sarong
    **b.** serape
    **c.** kilt
    **d.** kimono

**453.** femur : _____ :: fibula : calf
    **a.** foot
    **b.** thigh
    **c.** phalange
    **d.** muscle

**454.** mustang : _____ ::
    jaguar : cat
    **a.** dog
    **b.** horse
    **c.** fish
    **d.** bird

**455.** wed : _____ :: teem : meet
    **a.** engagement
    **b.** match
    **c.** rain
    **d.** dew

**456.** Bath : England ::
    _____ : France
    **a.** Lorca
    **b.** Lourdes
    **c.** Lucca
    **d.** Lucerne

**457.** V : X :: _____ : C
  a. I
  b. X
  c. L
  d. D

**458.** Ankara : Turkey ::
  _____ : Iraq
  a. Teheran
  b. Baghdad
  c. Istanbul
  d. Jordan

**459.** 18th Amendment :
  prohibition ::
  19th Amendment : _____
  a. speech
  b. suffrage
  c. slavery
  d. arms

**460.** Dickinson : _____ ::
  Dickens : novel
  a. novella
  b. poem
  c. song
  d. play

**461.** felt : _____ :: smelt : fish
  a. cloth
  b. nose
  c. sneeze
  d. scale

**462.** _____ : 1901 ::
  Lincoln : 1865
  a. Hoover
  b. Taft
  c. McKinley
  d. Ford

**463.** Bunker Hill : Revolutionary
  War :: _____ : Civil War
  a. Concord
  b. Alamo
  c. Boston Massacre
  d. Bull Run

**464.** 20 : 240 :: _____ : 180
  a. 18
  b. 12
  c. 15
  d. 6

**465.** El Cid : Spain ::
  Alexander : _____
  a. Alexandria
  b. Britain
  c. Germany
  d. Macedonia

**466.** de Soto : Spain ::
  Columbus : _____
  a. West Indies
  b. Italy
  c. Portugal
  d. Santa Maria

**467.** Iran : _____ ::
Germany : Prussia
  **a.** Syria
  **b.** Russia
  **c.** Iraq
  **d.** Persia

**468.** Swift : satirical ::
_____ : macabre
  **a.** Hemingway
  **b.** Fitzgerald
  **c.** Dos Passos
  **d.** Poe

**469.** Tokyo : Edo ::
_____ : Ceylon
  **a.** China
  **b.** Sri Lanka
  **c.** Mt. Fuji
  **d.** Vietnam

**470.** _____ : Southern ::
Hawthorne : Northern
  **a.** Melville
  **b.** Faulkner
  **c.** Kerouac
  **d.** Hemingway

**471.** Tuscan : Italy ::
Provençal : _____
  **a.** Switzerland
  **b.** Spain
  **c.** France
  **d.** England

**472.** Freud : psychoanalysis ::
_____ : genetics
  **a.** Mendel
  **b.** Pavlov
  **c.** Newton
  **d.** Copernicus

**473.** Fuji : Japan ::
Kilimanjaro : _____
  **a.** Africa
  **b.** China
  **c.** India
  **d.** Australia

**474.** 1 : Washington ::
_____ : Franklin
  **a.** 5
  **b.** 12
  **c.** 50
  **d.** 100

**475.** Van Buren : 8th ::
_____ : 16th
  **a.** Lincoln
  **b.** Jackson
  **c.** Adams
  **d.** Pierce

**476.** _____ : Gold Coast ::
Zimbabwe : Rhodesia
  **a.** Ghana
  **b.** California
  **c.** Sierra Leone
  **d.** Senegal

**477.** Saluki : _____ ::
Akita : Japan
a. London
b. Egypt
c. Chile
d. Spain

**478.** gold : Au :: silver : _____
a. Pb
b. Ag
c. Fe
d. Sn

**479.** peck : quart :: _____ : pint
a. kiss
b. gallon
c. glass
d. pound

**480.** Dryads : tree ::
Naiads : _____
a. rock
b. fire
c. sky
d. water

**481.** pound : United Kingdom ::
_____ : Costa Rica
a. franc
b. colón
c. peseta
d. dollar

**482.** Xerxes : Persia ::
Nebuchadnezzar : _____
a. Mesopotamia
b. Egypt
c. Babylon
d. Peru

**483.** Griffin : lion ::
Satyr : _____
a. owl
b. goat
c. wings
d. horse

**484.** Le Corbusier : architecture ::
Rodin : _____
a. symphony
b. sculpture
c. novel
d. automobile

**485.** Cyclops : 1 :: Argus : _____
a. 2
b. 5
c. 10
d. 100

**486.** Dalí : surrealism ::
Braque : _____
a. realism
b. pop
c. cubism
d. portraits

**487.** Nike : victory ::
_____ : hunt
a. Ares
b. Artemis
c. Hades
d. Hermes

**488.** Om : _____ ::
Ganges : India
**a.** Spain
**b.** Sweden
**c.** Hindu
**d.** Russia

**489.** Waterloo : Napoleon ::
Appomattox : _____
**a.** Lincoln
**b.** Grant
**c.** Lee
**d.** Sherman

**490.** Mohs : _____ ::
Richter : earthquake
**a.** intensity
**b.** damage
**c.** mineral
**d.** wind

**491.** _____ : highest ::
Death Valley : lowest
**a.** Mt. Rainier
**b.** Mauna Kea
**c.** Lake Champlain
**d.** Mt. McKinley

**492.** Samuel Clemens : Mark
Twain :: Mary Ann
Evans : _____
**a.** Eudora Welty
**b.** George Eliot
**c.** George Sand
**d.** Emily Brontë

**493.** Mississippi : Gulf of Mexico ::
Nile : _____
**a.** Indian Ocean
**b.** Mediterranean Sea
**c.** Atlantic Ocean
**d.** Persian Gulf

**494.** Crazy Horse : _____ ::
Cochise : Apache
**a.** Sioux
**b.** Inuit
**c.** Navajo
**d.** Custer

**495.** M : L :: C : _____
**a.** V
**b.** X
**c.** M
**d.** VI

**496.** 2nd : ordinal ::
_____ : cardinal
**a.** fraction
**b.** 3rd
**c.** 2
**d.** 1st

**497.** Neptune : Poseidon ::
Jupiter : _____
**a.** Nike
**b.** Mars
**c.** Zeus
**d.** Hera

**498.** Phoenix : bird ::
Pegasus : _____
  a. fish
  b. horse
  c. goat
  d. snake

**499.** Des Moines : Iowa ::
_____ : Texas
  a. Dallas
  b. Fort Worth
  c. Austin
  d. Cedar Rapids

**500.** Hawaii : 1959 ::
_____ : 1912
  a. New York
  b. South Carolina
  c. Arizona
  d. Maine

**501.** Sophocles : B.C. ::
_____ : A.D.
  a. Euripedes
  b. Pindar
  c. Dante
  d. Virgil

# Answers

**451.** **b.** 30 is half of 60, and 1/3 is half of 2/3.

**452.** **b.** A sari is traditional clothing worn in India, and a **serape** is traditional clothing worn in Mexico.

**453.** **b.** The femur is located in the **thigh**, and the fibula is located in the calf.

**454.** **b.** A mustang is a type of **horse**, and a jaguar is a type of cat.

**455.** **d.** Wed is a palindrome for **dew**, and teem is a palindrome for meet.

**456.** **b.** Restorative waters are found in Bath, England, as well as in **Lourdes**, France.

**457.** **c.** In Roman numerals, V (5) is half of X (10), and **L** (50) is half of C (100).

**458.** **b.** Ankara is the capital of Turkey, and **Baghdad** is the capital of Iraq.

**459.** **b.** The 18th Amendment dealt with prohibition, and the 19th dealt with **suffrage**.

**460.** **b.** Emily Dickinson was known as a **poet**, and Charles Dickens was a novelist.

**461.** **a.** Felt is a type of **cloth**, and smelt is a type of fish.

**462.** **c.** President McKinley was **assassinated** in 1901, and President Lincoln was assassinated in 1865.

**463.** **d.** Bunker Hill was a battle site in the Revolutionary War, and **Bull Run** was a battle site in the Civil War.

**464.** **c.** 20 times 12 is 240, and **15** times 12 is 180.

**465.** **d.** El Cid was a military leader from Spain, and Alexander was a military leader of **Macedonia**.

**466.** **b.** de Soto was a Spanish navigator, and Columbus was an **Italian** navigator.

**467.** **d.** Iran was formerly called **Persia**, and Germany was formerly called Prussia.

**468.** **d.** Jonathan Swift was known as a satirical writer, and **Edgar Allan Poe** was known for his macabre writing.

**469.** **b.** Tokyo was formerly known as Edo, and **Sri Lanka** was formerly known as Ceylon.

**470.** **b.** **William Faulkner** is known as a Southern writer, and Nathaniel Hawthorne is known as a Northern writer.

**471.** **c.** Tuscan relates to a region of Italy, and **Provençal** relates to a region of France.

**472.** **a.** Freud is considered the father of psychoanalysis, and **Mendel** is considered the father of genetics.

**473.** **a.** Fuji is the highest mountain in Japan, and Kilimanjaro is the highest mountain in **Tanzania**.

**474.** **d.** George Washington's portrait is on the one-dollar bill, and Benjamin Franklin's is on the **100**.

**475.** **a.** Martin Van Buren was the 8th president, and **Abraham Lincoln** was the 16th.

**476.** **a.** **Ghana** was formerly called the Gold Coast, and Zimbabwe was formerly called Rhodesia.

**477.** **b.** The Saluki is a breed of dog from **Egypt**, and the Akita is a breed of dog from Japan.

**478.** **b.** On the periodic table of elements, the symbol for gold is Au, and the symbol for silver is **Ag**.

**479.** **b.** A peck is a unit of measure equal to 8 quarts, and a **gallon** is a unit of measurement equal to 8 pints.

**480.** **d.** The Dryads were mythical tree nymphs, and the Naiads were mythical **water** nymphs.

**481.** **b.** The pound is the unit of currency of the United Kingdom, and the **colón** is the unit of currency in Costa Rica.

**482.** **c.** Xerxes was the ancient king of Persia, and Nebuchadnezzar was the ancient king of **Babylon**.

**483.** **b.** A Griffin is a mythical creature with the body of a lion, and a Satyr has the body of a **goat**.

**484.** **b.** Le Corbusier was a French architect, and Rodin was a French **sculptor**.

**485.** **d.** Cyclops was the mythical creature with one eye, and Argus was a creature with **100** eyes.

**486.** **c.** Salvador Dalí is known as a surrealist painter, and Georges Braque is known as a **cubist**.

**487.** **b.** Nike is the goddess of victory, and **Artemis** is the goddess of the hunt.

**488.** **d.** The Om is a river in **Russia**, and the Ganges is a river in India.

**489.** **c.** Waterloo was the site of Napoleon's defeat, and Appomattox was the site of General **Lee's** defeat.

**490.** **c.** The Mohs scale is used to measure the hardness of **minerals**, and the Richter scale is used to measure the intensity of earthquakes.

**491.** d. **Mt. McKinley** is the highest point in the United States, and Death Valley is the lowest.

**492.** b. Samuel Clemens wrote under the name Mark Twain, and Mary Ann Evans wrote under the name **George Eliot**.

**493.** b. The Mississippi River flows into the Gulf of Mexico, and the Nile River flows into the **Mediterranean Sea**.

**494.** a. Crazy Horse was the leader of the **Sioux**, and Cochise was the leader of the Apache.

**495.** a. M (1000) divided by L (50) is 20, as is C (100) divided by **V** (5).

**496.** c. 2nd is an example of an ordinal number, and **2** is an example of a cardinal number.

**497.** c. Neptune is the Roman name of the Greek god Poseidon, and Jupiter is the Roman name of the Greek god **Zeus**.

**498.** b. Phoenix is a mythical bird, and Pegasus is a mythical **horse**.

**499.** c. Des Moines is the capital of Iowa, and **Austin** is the capital of Texas.

**500.** c. Hawaii became a state in 1959, and **Arizona** became a state in 1912.

**501.** c. Sophocles was born in B.C., and **Dante** was born and lived A.D.

# SKILL BUILDER IN FOCUS

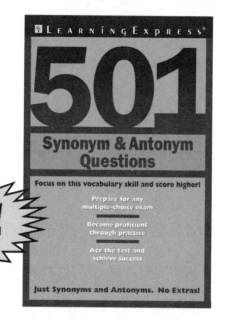

**ISBN: 1-57685-4423-X**
**128 pages**
**7 x 10**
**AUGUST 2002**

# 501 Synonym and Antonym Questions

**Master this vocabulary skill and score higher!**

**Achieve maximum results with proven practice**

**Build test-taking confidence—fast**

**Great for the SAT, GRE, GMAT—
and other standardized tests**

**Start thinking of words in terms of other words
with similar or opposite meanings**

**Pinpoint exact word definitions and
become aware of secondary word meanings**

**Learn to switch gears from synonym questions to
antonym questions, avoiding careless mistakes**

**Assess your true vocabulary level and
put yourself on the path to improvement**

# Focus *FAST* on Synonyms and Antonyms

# SKILL BUILDER IN FOCUS

ISBN: 1-57685-424-8
288 pages
7 x 10
AUGUST 2002

## 501 Algebra Questions

**Master this math skill and score higher!**

**Achieve maximum results with proven practice**

**Build test-taking confidence—fast**

**Great practice for the SAT, GRE, GMAT—
and other standardized tests**

**Learn math concepts and properties**

**Work with algebraic expressions and integers**

**Multiply and factor polynomials, use quadratic
formulas, and avoid careless mistakes**

**Assess your true algebra competency level
and put yourself on the path to improvement**

## Focus *FAST* on Algebra

# SKILL BUILDER IN FOCUS

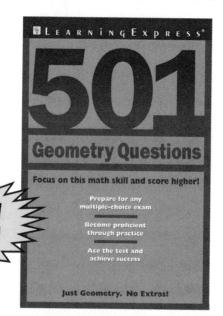

ISBN: 1-57685-425-6
288 pages
7 x 10
AUGUST 2002

## 501 Geometry Questions

**Master this math skill and score higher!**

**Achieve maximum results with proven practice**

**Build test-taking confidence—fast**

**Great for the SAT, GRE, GMAT—
and other standardized tests**

**Learn math concepts and properties,
including trigonometry basics**

**Work with angles and lines, identify shapes,
determine ratios, proportion, perimeter,
and surface measures**

**Assess your true geometry competency level
and put yourself on the path to improvement**

## Focus *FAST* on Geometry

# SKILL BUILDER IN FOCUS
## coming in Winter 2003

# 501 Quantitative Comparison Questions
ISBN: 1-57685-434-5 ▪ 224 pages ▪ 7 x 10 ▪ January

# 501 Writing Prompts
ISBN: 1-57685-438-8 ▪ 128 pages ▪ 7 x 10 ▪ February

# 501 Math Word Problems
ISBN: 1-57685-439-6 ▪ 224 pages ▪ 7 x 10 ▪ March

**Master these skills and score higher!**

**Achieve maximum results with proven practice**

**Build test-taking confidence—fast**

**Great for the SAT, GRE, GMAT— and other standardized tests**

# Focus *FAST* on the Skills You Need to Pass the Test